THE LABOUR PARTY IN PERSPECTIVE

THE LABOUR PARTY IN PERSPECTIVE

by

C. R. ATTLEE

LONDON
VICTOR GOLLANCZ LTD
1937

Printed in Great Britain by
The Camelot Press Ltd., London and Southampton

CONTENTS

Chapter I.	Introductory	*page* 7
II.	Historical Retrospect	33
III.	Trade Union and Co-operative Movements	62
IV.	Constitution	85
V.	Labour Party Method	113
VI.	Socialist Objective	137
VII.	Short Programme	166
VIII.	Foreign Policy	199
IX.	The Commonwealth and the Empire	228
X.	Labour and Defence	248
XI.	Prospect	273

CHAPTER I

INTRODUCTORY

SOME THIRTY YEARS AGO, when I was a young barrister just down from Oxford, I engaged in various forms of social work in East London. The condition of the people in that area as I saw them at close quarters led me to study their causes and to reconsider the assumptions of the social class to which I belonged. I became an enthusiastic convert to Socialism. I joined the Fabian Society and the Independent Labour Party and became a member of my trade union, the National Union of Clerks. For many years I worked as a rank and file member of the movement, taking my share of the work of branch activities and propaganda meetings at street corners. I shared the hopes and disappointments incidental to Socialist work in what was then a very backward area.

After the war, as Mayor and Alderman of a Borough Council and as a Poor Law Guardian, I had a full experience of municipal work. I was then elected to Parliament. Circumstances have called me to occupy a position of high responsibility in the movement. Throughout these years I have never wavered in my faith in the cause of Socialism. I have never lost my early enthusiasm. I have never doubted that the Labour Party, whatever faults or failings it may have, is the only practical instrument in this country for the attainment of a new order of society.

I have seen the Party grow until its adherents in the electorate number over eight millions. I have seen the little group of thirty Labour members, united on the basis of independent working-class representation, transformed into a Labour Party in the House of Commons of nearly three hundred men and women, comprising individuals of widely differing social backgrounds, but united in their support of Socialism, which has become the avowed aim of the movement.

During all these years there has never been a time when there were not questionings in the ranks and suggestions of breakaway movements. There has never been a lack of candid criticism of the policy and achievements of the official Labour Party. I have seen a good many leaders of revolt arise, and very often, to use an expressive phrase, I have seen them meet themselves coming back. I have myself often shared in these criticisms and questionings, and have been discontented with decisions taken, although I have accepted them. But despite rumblings on the Right and denunciations on the Left, the Party has continued on its way, steadily growing in numbers and influence. Even the desertion of prominent leaders at a critical moment failed to do more than check its advance numerically, while it strengthened and purified its faith and purpose.

There is to-day as much criticism of the Labour Party as ever, especially from those whose enthusiastic desires make official policy and action appear too slow. I am glad that this should be so. Self-criticism is a healthy thing so long as it does not lead to a paralysis of the will. I should not like to see Labour a party on the pattern of those which exist in corporate States, where exact obedience and loyalty to a leader stifle free thought and destroy individual initiative. In a party of the Left there should always be room for differences of opinion and emphasis. If the Party is to renew itself by drawing on the rising generation, there will necessarily be disagreements due to the different environment in which the young have grown up.

On the other hand, there is a danger that a party may be so concerned about its own health that it becomes a political valetudinarian, incapable of taking an active part in affairs. It may discuss its own internal condition to such an extent that it disgusts all those with whom it comes in contact.

A new generation is growing up in this country which knows little of the conditions in which the Labour Party started. To them there has always been a Labour Party. It is a familiar feature in the political landscape. The controversy between Socialism and Capitalism is the dominant public question of the day, while the old division between Liberal and Conservative, which is still such a vivid memory to their parents, is as much a part of history as the contests between Whigs and Tories. There are many thousands who have been brought up in Socialist homes. To them Socialism is orthodoxy. They hardly understand the feelings of us older ones to whom the emergence of the Labour Party as a great political force is still something of a miracle, and to whom the fight for Socialism still partakes of the nature of a forlorn attack upon the serried ranks of the supporters of things as they are. They see before their eyes the great experiment in Socialist Russia. They see a community actually putting into operation the Socialist economic system which their predecessors of twenty years ago could only contemplate as a distant dream.

Between this younger generation and the veterans of the movement lies the deep gulf of the Great War. Many of the assumptions of the pre-war years have passed away and it requires an effort to recall them. In many respects, therefore, there has been a change in outlook which has affected, not only the supporters, but the opponents of Socialism. To the majority of the members of the House of Commons of 1907 the ordinary assumptions of an intelligent young Conservative of to-day would seem rank blasphemy, and his views on the Capitalist system sheer infidelity.

There is, therefore, a danger that the older and younger generations may fail to arrive at an understanding. There are always some old men who remain young and find no difficulty in entering into the spirit of a new era. There are always some young people who can appreciate the attitude of mind of their elders, but, to most of us, to do either the one or the other means a constant and serious effort. It is, therefore, perhaps useful that one who belongs neither to the old pioneers nor to the young entrants, but is a survivor of the generation which lost so many of its members in the Great War, should look backwards and forwards and try to see the Labour Party in perspective. It may be that this task would be better done by one who is able to sit back and from a position of detachment and leisure survey the past, the present, and the future, than by a man engaged from day to day in the pressing problems that beset the leader of a great political party. It may be, on the other hand, that close contact with everyday realities and constant intercourse with those who are active in the ranks of Labour may give a better perspective. It may, on the one hand, prevent too much reminiscence and the over-idealisation of the past which comes to those whose work is done, and, on the other, check vain imaginings about the future, wherein the goal to be reached is clearly set out, while the path that leads to it, and the obstacles in the way, are only faintly indicated.

This, then, is my intention in the present volume. I want, in the first place, to show the Labour Party in its historical setting as an expression conditioned in place and time of the urge for Socialism. I want to show it as a characteristic example of British methods, and as the outcome of British political instincts. I want to examine its characteristics, to show how it functions, and to disprove or approve the criticisms passed upon it. Finally, I want to consider its future in the light of present-day conditions. In this volume I shall necessarily be expressing my own views. I am not writing an exposition of official Party policy, although I think that what I write is in accord with it. I believe that there is a far wider agreement in the movement than is always realised. Probably every member of the Party will find in what I say something with which he disagrees. One aspect of policy will be unduly stressed in his view; another will not be sufficiently emphasised. This is natural. I write as an individual, and the perspective is my own. My desire, however, is to give, as far as I am able, the views of the ordinary rank and file member of the Party. During all my years in the movement, what has impressed me most is that its strength depends, not on the brilliance of individuals, but on the quality of the rank and file. It is the self-sacrifice, idealism, and character of the men and women who do the everyday work of the Party up and down the country that makes me hopeful of the future. It is not the theories so much as the lives of those who advocate them which really count in the progress of a great movement.

The Labour Party may be considered under two aspects, as part of a great international movement and as a British political party.

Taking a broad survey of history, we can discern beneath surface differences great movements which affect all peoples who are living at the same general level of civilisation and are subject to the play of the same economic forces. These movements express themselves differently in particular countries in accordance with the history and conditions obtaining there and the mental and social habits of the people inhabiting them. A great movement is like a tide. It will flow later in one place than in another. It may come in steadily and silently on a low sandy shore, but run violently against the rocks elsewhere. It may be checked by an adverse wind or be deflected by cross-currents, but it is the same tide. The shores against which it flows have been affected by the forces of the past.

Thus during the nineteenth century there was a great movement which was called Liberal. In Great Britain it was in the main peaceful, and represented the sweeping away of old restrictions and the accession to power of the middle class. In France its course was marked by revolutionary outbreaks. In Russia it was driven underground, and expressed itself in terrorist outrages. Its manifestations were widely different, but it was essentially the same spirit.

Behind this liberating idea was the economic force of industrialism striving against the power of the landed interest. There were many conflicting cross-currents. Where the dominant economic interest coincided with oppression by another race, Liberalism combined with nationalism. Where the dominant social class was allied to a particular form of religion, the struggle took on a sectarian basis. Viewed from the standpoint of a particular nation, the contest seemed to be local, but we can now, looking back, discern the unity underlying the diversity.

Liberalism—or, rather, Liberal Capitalism—was the dominant influence of the nineteenth century. Its expression varied from country to country. Its methods were adapted to circumstances and to the national character in each country. Its adherents often rejected spiritual kinship with those whose methods they disapproved. The complacent British Liberal was offended by the excesses of foreign revolutionaries. There was little unity in the attack against the common enemy.

The dominant issue of the twentieth century is Socialism. The Labour Party is the expression in Great Britain of a world-wide movement. In every country in the world where modern Capitalism has developed, there is to be found in some form or another a revolt of those who suffer from its conditions and reject its assumptions. Wherever the economic system has developed in such a way that the instruments of production are in the hands of a possessing class, while the workers own little or nothing but their labour, a Socialist movement will be found. The form of the revolt will differ in every country. There is no sealed pattern for the social revolution.

Socialism is not the invention of an individual. essentially the outcome of economic and social conditions. The evils that Capitalism brings differ in intensity in different countries, but, the root cause of the trouble once discerned, the remedy is seen to be the same by thoughtful men and women. The cause is the private ownership of the means of life; the remedy is public ownership. The essentials of Socialism have been well stated by Bertrand Russell:

"Socialism means the common ownership of land and capital together with a democratic form of government. It involves production for use not profit, and distribution of the product either equally to all or, at any rate, with only such inequalities as are definitely in the public interest. It involves the abolition of all unearned wealth and of all private control over the means of livelihood of the workers. To be fully realised it must be international."

The means adopted in order to attain this objective depend on the circumstances of each country.

Where there is no political freedom and no liberty of combination, inevitably there will be a resort to violence. The achievements of the Liberal epoch have not been realised. Personal and political liberty have to be sought in face of the armed force of tyranny. Where there is no liberty the movement will be driven underground, as in pre-war Russia and in the Fascist States of to-day, and will exhibit characteristics of underground movements. Where government has always been synonymous with oppression, there will be a tendency towards anarchy, as in Spain. Where national liberty has not been achieved, Socialism may be submerged for a time under Nationalism. Where there is rule by priests, it may become violently anti-clerical. Where there is no tradition of tolerance and no training in democracy, it may become authoritarian and intolerant.

Where, however, there is personal and political freedom, a democratic constitution, and a wide franchise, there is the possibility of achieving Socialist ends by constitutional methods, and political action will be the rule.

An examination of the Socialist movements throughout the world will show how their form is conditioned by their circumstances. The broad division is dictated by the presence or absence of the practice and traditions of democracy. A large number of European countries hardly know the meaning of the word. Their whole history has been one of failures to make democracy work, with consequent relapses into dictatorship of one kind and another. The Socialist movement has proceeded in those countries on "crisis" lines. On the other hand, in Western Europe, where bourgeois democracy has been long established, the Socialist movement has been constitutional and has grown steadily. In the Scandinavian countries, in Belgium, Holland, and France, strong political parties have been built up which have in some cases attained to, and in other cases shared, power. They have gained considerable advantages for the workers. They have built up semi-Socialist oases within the Capitalist system. They have modified the rigours of Capitalism. The governing classes have made concessions to the workers owing to the comparative prosperity of these countries.

Sweden has afforded perhaps the most remarkable example of the successful development of Socialism through constitutional means that is to be found in Europe. While it is still far from being a Socialist country, there has been a wide development of State control and ownership of finance and industry. The State owns the central bank, the air lines, and the overwhelming proportion of the railway system. It is the owner of some ten million acres of forests, which it exploits with considerable success. It has established a network of power stations, and is the chief distributor of electric power in the country. It owns the mining rights to the largest iron ore deposits in the country, and exploits them in conjunction with a private company. It has a monopoly of the importation of all unprocessed tobacco and the manufacture and wholesale distribution of cigars and cigarettes. Side by side with these semi-State industries there is one of the biggest Co-operative movements in the world, which carries on some 20 per cent of all the wholesale and retail trade of the country, and has, in addition, a large number of factories.

The results of these developments in co-operation and State ownership are to be seen in the relative prosperity of the Swedish worker. Sweden has led the way in the development of old age pensions, and has been responsible for some of the best housing schemes that are to be found anywhere. Throughout the depression, unemployment never reached anything like the proportions that it attained in other countries. All this has been achieved without any bloodshed and with the minimum possible of friction. Regarded as an instalment of further developments towards the Socialist goal, it can indeed be said to present a remarkable example of the use of constitutional methods.

This last year, however, has afforded by far the most interesting development in constitutional Socialism that we have yet seen. I refer, of course, to the work of the newly elected Labour Government in New Zealand. Within twelve months this Government has changed New Zealand from a country suffering under all the evils attendant on Capitalism, with a high ratio of unemployment and considerable poverty among large sections of workers, to one in which there exists security of living for all, together with a steadily rising tide of prosperity. The central banking system has been taken out of the hands of private individuals and made into a national concern. A generous system of old age pensions has been introduced; a forty-hour week has been established, together with a minimum wage that is far in excess of anything previously known in New Zealand. The export of dairy products, which is the largest single export in the country, has been taken over by the State, which pays a guaranteed price to the farmer for all the produce that it buys. All this, and more, has been done within the first year of office of a constitutionally elected Labour Government in a British Dominion. The end of its first period of office should see New Zealand well on the road to Socialism, without a vestige of dictatorship and with full democratic rights preserved.

The British Labour Party is an expression of the Socialist movement adapted to British conditions. It is also a political movement of the British people in line of succession to many others. The dominant note of the history of this country is its continuity. It is our national habit to look for precedents in the past for every step forward which we make. We trace our liberties back to the struggles against kings, barons, and bishops. We trace the growth of political and personal liberty back to Magna Charta and Habeas Corpus. We mark the widening of freedom and its extension from one class to another. The instruments by which that freedom has been achieved differ widely in character. Sometimes it has been a king checking the tyranny of feudal barons. Sometimes it has been nobles and gentry curbing the power of the Crown. Now it has been the Church protecting the people. At another time the people have resisted the pretensions of ecclesiastics.

INTRODUCTORY

The battleground of freedom has changed from time to time. The fortresses to be captured have been various. The autocratic power of the king, the dominance in the legislature of the few, have been overthrown. Rights of free speech, freedom of conscience, and the right to take part in government have all been asserted, but at the back of all these contests for political power has been the desire to use that power for economic ends.

The immediate predecessors of the Labour Party were the Liberals. They sought to free the individual from the power of the State. They believed that economic liberty meant political freedom. Realising that British liberty was essentially the liberty of the man of property, they thought that under free competition, and with a wide distribution of individual property, this could be achieved.

The dominant issue throughout the nineteenth century, as it seemed to most thinking men and women, was political liberty. The issue of the twentieth century is economic freedom and social equality. Socialists realised that political and personal liberty must be supplemented by economic liberty. That liberty is not to be obtained individually, but collectively. The change in the scale of industrial operations from a small group of individuals working with simple tools to immense regiments of men and women co-operating in the use of vast machines driven by mechanical power has made it impossible to achieve liberty by an extension of private property to the many. Collective control of the great forces released by modern science is the only way in which to obtain freedom. Collective security is the only form which is possible.

The Labour Party is the inheritor of the achievements of those who fought for liberty in the past. It looks back with sympathy, not only to the political struggles of former days, but to the economic contests. It sees behind the political fight the striving of the workers for their rights. It is determined to preserve the liberties which it has inherited and to add to them. Its aim is the same as that of those who have gone before. It seeks to free the human spirit, but its immediate objectives are those which modern conditions dictate.

It is necessary to bear in mind this historical position of the Labour Party. It is not the creation of a theorist. It does not propagate some theory produced in another country. It is seeking to show the people of Great Britain that the Socialism which it preaches is what the country requires in order in modern conditions to realise to the full the genius of the nation.

For the development of a democratic Socialist movement two things are required: first, the existence of a developed Capitalist system, and second, the emergence of someone who will make a synthesis of the discontents of the wage-earners and relate them to a common cause. For a Socialist movement to develop into a constitutional political party there must be a democratic constitution, with a franchise sufficiently wide to make possible the achievement of political power by the masses.

To understand why the Socialist movement developed in Great Britain on its own distinctive lines, and why the Labour Party came into existence at a particular time, it is necessary to consider the conditions which obtained in the first half of the nineteenth century. The Labour Party is the youngest of the three great British working-class movements. It followed long after the Trade Union and Co-operative movements had become strong. To us this seems normal, but in many countries the organisation of producers and consumers has resulted from the purposeful working of Socialist parties. This order of precedence is the result of many factors which must be examined.

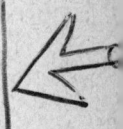

The Capitalist system developed earlier in Great Britain than in other countries, and consequently the organisation of the workers began sooner. In the early years of the nineteenth century the Capitalist system was not fully developed. Industrial units were still comparatively small, and owned by small masters. Industry was not highly integrated. It was a period of transition. In such conditions the interests of particular sections of workers tend to override and obscure in their minds the common concern of the whole class. Advantages may be won for exclusive groups whose skill gives them bargaining power. Differences of status between the workers themselves loom large. The possibilities of individual advancement militate against solidarity.

Nevertheless the evils of Capitalism in the first half of the nineteenth century were so great that there seemed the possibility of a revolution by the workers. A prophet was at hand in Robert Owen, who exposed the nature of Capitalism and pointed to Socialism as the remedy. It might have been expected that at this time a great political Socialist movement would have arisen in this country. There was a period, indeed, in which there seemed the possibility of a violent revolution in Britain, but the moment passed. Revolutionary trade unionism died out. Revolutionary Chartism was, in effect, superseded by other movements, such as the agitation against the Corn Laws, which made a more immediate appeal. The workers of Britain turned to more limited and, as it seemed, more practical objectives. The Trade Union movement, the Co-operative movement, and factory legislation owed much to the inspiration of Owen. They attacked Capitalism from within, and sought either to act as a check on its excesses or to build up a new society within the old. But the impulse for the abolition of the system as a whole died away. Revolution gave place to reform. The British workman politically became a unit in the general body of Liberalism. Organised Labour set itself to extract what it could from Parliament by bringing pressure to bear on both the old parties in the State.

But there was another reason for the slow development of a Socialist movement in this country. We to-day are accustomed to see in political life the domination of the economic issue, and it is an effort for us to realise how throughout the nineteenth century political issues such as franchise reform or Irish Home Rule absorbed the political thought of the workers. Still less are we able in these days to appreciate how important were then considered the quarrels between the various political sects. The nineteenth century, which seems to our young men and women dull, stuffy, and Victorian, was a time when every kind of belief was being challenged and all kinds of struggles were proceeding. It is idle to dismiss these as of no importance because they seem so to us. They were important to the men and women of that time. In this Victorian age there were many prophets preaching various gospels, and this must be borne in mind if one wishes to discover the springs of action of the Labour movement and to appreciate its character. The ideas which called the pioneers to the service of the Socialist movement were very varied. They were not the followers of a single gospel of one prophet. They did not accept one revelation as inspired. It is this which distinguishes the British Socialist movement from many of those on the Continent. Predominantly the parties on the Continent have been built on the writings of Karl Marx. Around his teachings the movement has grown. Different interpretations have been put upon his creed. In some countries other powerful influences have been at work, and the characters of his apostles and the circumstances of the countries to which they belong have necessarily caused differences in the method pursued by particular parties, but they have this in common—that they were formed as definite Socialist movements, inspired by the word revealed to Marx.

In Britain the history of the movement has been entirely different. Widely diffused as his influence has been, the number of those who accepted Marxism as a creed has always been small. The number of those who have entered the Socialist movement as the direct result of his teaching has been but a fraction of the whole. One must seek the inspiration of the majority of British Socialists in other directions.

Leaving aside Owen and the early pioneers, I

think that the first place in the influences that built up the Socialist movement must be given to religion. England in the nineteenth century was still a nation of Bible readers. To put the Bible into the hands of an Englishman is to do a very dangerous thing. He will find there material which may send him out as a preacher of some religious, social, or economic doctrine. The large number of religious sects in this country, and the various tenets that many of them hold, illustrate this.

The Bible is full of revolutionary teaching, and it is not surprising that, in a country where thought is free, many men and women have drawn from it the support which they needed for their instinctive revolt against the inhuman conditions which Capitalism brings. I think that probably the majority of those who have built up the Socialist movement in this country have been adherents of the Christian religion—and not merely adherents, but enthusiastic members of some religious body. There are probably more texts from the Bible enunciated from Socialist platforms than from those of all other parties. Not only the adherents of dissenting bodies whose less privileged position inclined them to take a Left Wing line in politics, but also many clergy and laymen of the Established Church, found that the Capitalist system was incompatible with Christianity. It is significant that the gap between the end of Owenism and the birth of the Social Democratic Federation is filled by the Christian Socialist movement of Kingsley and Maurice. Here one sees a feature which distinguishes the British movement from most of those abroad. In no other country has Christianity become converted to Socialism to such an extent as in Britain. In no other Socialist movement has Christian thought had such a powerful leavening effect. It is possible in Britain for a parson to declare himself a Communist and for millions of faithful Catholics to support the Labour Party. It may be noted as a factor in building the British Labour movement on broad foundations that so many of the adherents of the Catholic Faith in Britain come from Ireland, where a creed of political and economic revolt has been inculcated into a Catholic population. The British Labour movement owes much to these men and women, who brought over from their own country their hatred of oppression.

The Labour Party necessarily differs from those Continental countries where Socialists found themselves faced by a Church either closely bound up with the State or with property or class interests, and inimical to liberty of thought. Where, as in many countries, the workers in the formative years of the Socialist movement were attached to a dogmatic faith which controlled every phase of their lives, it was natural that the movement of revolt should be anti-clerical. To meet the conditions there was set up a dogmatism equally narrow and exclusive. The divisions between blacks and reds extending into every activity became absolute. Neither side could influence the other any more than can two contending armies entrenched against each other. Such a division undoubtedly gives great driving-force and cohesion to a movement, but it creates such a fissure in the body politic that the result is either stalemate or revolution. Neither can advance or retreat. In Britain, on the other hand, where political and religious differences do not coincide, there is a constant broadening owing to contact.

There were many other influences at work in the preparation of the ground for the seed of Socialism. The denunciation of industrialists and of Manchester School Economics by Carlyle and Ruskin, and the literature of exposure of social abuses of which Dickens's works are the outstanding example, had their effect. Later the work of those who preached land reform, and especially the campaigns of Henry George, were instrumental in creating a receptivity to Socialist ideas in many minds. From different points of view, humanitarian, artistic, and economic, the flood of criticism of the existing order grew throughout the nineteenth century. It affected the adherents of the old political parties, but it was a long time before a political Socialist movement became really effective. I shall deal in the next chapter with the actual formation of the Labour Party and with the work of the Socialist Societies which helped to create it. In this chapter I am only indicating the particular characteristics of the British Socialist movement.

It naturally follows, however, from the heterogeneity of the sources from which the movement drew its inspiration, that the Labour Party has always comprised people of very various outlooks, and that its note has always been one of comprehensiveness. The natural British tendency to heresy and dissent has prevented the formation of a code of rigid Socialist orthodoxy. Those who have sought to impose one have always failed to make real headway and have remained sects rather than political parties. As in religion, so in politics and economics, the Briton claims the right to think for himself.

A further characteristic of the British movement has been its practicality. It has never consisted of a body of theorists or of revolutionaries who were so absorbed in Utopian dreams that they were unwilling to deal with the actualities of everyday life. From the first, British Socialists have taken their share wherever possible in the responsibility of Government. The British system of local Government has proved to be an excellent training-ground. Long before there were more than a handful of Labour members in Parliament, Socialists had won their way on to local councils and were influencing administration. By showing what could be done in a small sphere they were able to convert many sceptical workers who would only believe what they saw in being. The work of the Fabian Society in particular inspired many to bring about an immense change in the attitude of local authorities towards social problems. It is hardly realised by many in the movement to-day how much was accomplished by men like Lansbury and Crooks in revolutionising the ideas of the people with regard to Poor Law administration.

Looking back over the past thirty years, the most striking feature in the mentality of the people of this country of all classes has been the change in their attitude to social questions. The assumptions have altered. Propositions indignantly rejected in the nineties have now passed into common acceptance. I can well remember the time when it was assumed that everyone unemployed, was so, through his own fault. The fact that to-day unemployment is realised to be in the majority of cases a misfortune due to the maladjustment of the economic machine instead of a failure of character is mainly due to Socialists.

Therefore in judging the work of the Labour Party it is essential to bear in mind not only direct, but indirect, results of its work. Those who count progress only in terms of seats won and of the growth of the numbers of the professed adherents of the Party miss the real significance of what has happened. The outstanding thing is not so much the growth in the strength of the forces which attack the citadel of Capitalism as in the loss of the outworks, the crumbling of the foundations, and the loss of morale of the garrison. The character of Socialist propaganda has changed during the last thirty years because to-day speakers can start their arguments from premises which were denied in the earlier period. The emphasis to-day is less on destruction and more on construction. The task is harder. It is not enough to-day to denounce Capitalism and then leave Socialism to a few general principles. The modern Socialist must be able to show the immediate steps which Socialists will take when they achieve power. The vision of the future has now to be translated into practical action. The Short Programme issued by the Labour Party is the proof of this change.

CHAPTER II

HISTORICAL RETROSPECT

I HAVE ENDEAVOURED in the last chapter to indicate the particular conditions which have given to the British Labour movement its distinctive character. I now wish to trace in outline the origin and growth of the Labour Party. I have shown that there were in existence in this country the conditions which called for Socialism and the ideas which revealed to the workers their discontents and showed the remedy. There were many people who drew attention to the evils of Capitalism. There were throughout the nineteenth century many who, feeling the prick of conscience, strove by their individual action to remedy the ills which they saw, but the creation of the Labour Party was due to two things—the active Socialist propaganda of hundreds of men and women who sacrificed themselves freely for an ideal, and the needs of the organised workers who recognised that the methods of strikes and mutual assistance must be supplemented by parliamentary action. The British Socialist movement has produced brilliant individuals such as

Cp

Robert Blatchford, who did great service in converting the workers to Socialism. It has from time to time produced numerous groups or sects whose adherents preached particular varieties of the Socialist gospel. There were, however, three organisations which have been the main contributors to the spread of Socialist thought in this country and to the creation of a political Socialist movement. All three have their own characteristics.

The first was the Social Democratic Federation. Founded by H. M. Hyndman it was based definitely on the teaching of Karl Marx. It tended to be somewhat doctrinaire and to preserve an exclusiveness and rigidity which was not altogether in harmony with the character of the people of this country. Its adherents showed immense courage at a time when Socialist propagandists were often met with physical force. It lived adventurously, and its members took a prominent part in the industrial struggles of the eighties and nineties. Its pioneer work was invaluable, but it failed to create a mass movement. Its membership remained small.

The Fabian Society, essentially a middle-class body, was the antithesis of the S.D.F. Rejecting the frontal attack, it worked by permeation. Sidney Webb and his colleagues worked in the field of ideas. They inserted into the amorphous mass of Left opinion a Socialist leaven which worked with ever increasing results. They set themselves to translate Socialism into the terms of everyday life. They developed theory, it is true, but far more they exposed facts and provided the active propagandist with his ammunition. They took Socialism away from the realm of abstraction and showed how its principles could be applied to the actual, existing institutions of society.

The third organisation, the Independent Labour Party, was the creation of Keir Hardie. Unlike the S.D.F., it was inclusive and undogmatic. Like the S.D.F., it worked at the street corner and in the mill, the factory, the mine, and the Trade Union branch. Its active members brought to their task an apostolic enthusiasm. It had something of the quality of a religious body. Its particular contribution to British Socialism was its recognition that the Trade Union movement, although dominated largely by Liberals, was yet the essential basis for a working-class political party. It was a practical expression of the slogan, " Workers, Unite." It aimed at detaching from their allegiance to Capitalist parties the workers who were already united on a class basis. At the high-water mark of its activity, it was the most lively political force in the country. Week in, week out, from thousands of platforms its gospel was proclaimed. It attracted members of the middle class as well as workers. It is difficult for those who know the

I.L.P. in its decadence as a sect to realise the joyful fellowship it was in its great days.

These three great organisations, working in their various ways on public opinion, were the active forces of Socialism at the time when the Labour Party was being born, but they did not themselves develop into a great political party.

It is characteristic of the British Labour movement that the origin of the Labour Party is to be found in fact rather than in theory. The Labour Party was originally the by-product of Trade Union activity. The fact of the unity of working class interests on particular matters of common concern which required to be dealt with by State action led to the first beginnings of Labour activity in the political field. The movement which resulted in the return of the first Trade Union representatives to the House of Commons in 1874 was far from being revolutionary, and the men themselves were not Socialists. They entered Parliament, not to overthrow the Capitalist system, but to win for the workers certain definite reforms. Apart from their specific demands on Labour questions, they formed part of the Liberal Party.

It is, perhaps, difficult for the young Socialist of to-day to appreciate at its full value the work that Thomas Burt and Alexander Macdonald, and the men who joined them later, accomplished. It is not easy to carry one's mind back to the time when working men were definitely considered to belong to the "lower classes." Their advent into "the best club in the world," the House of Commons, was an intrusion. These men showed that working men could hold their own in the most exacting assembly in the world, and brought there for the first time the outlook and mental background of the working class.

The group of men who were later known as Lib-Labs were men of character and standing, and their advice and example naturally had a powerful effect on the minds of the average Trade Unionist. Their influence was for many years a powerful obstacle to the formation of an independent Labour political movement on a Socialist basis. Although from 1885 the Socialist leaven was working among the organised workers, it failed to have effect. All the sentiment which to-day gathers round the idea of the Popular Front was on the side of the Liberal Party. To attempt to run Labour candidates against Liberal Capitalists was splitting the progressive forces. Against this the Social Democratic Federation struggled in vain, while the Fabians, with their policy of permeation, were an influence on the side of the unity of the progressive forces.

It was the emergence of the third Socialist body, the Independent Labour Party, which was the effective force in turning the Trade Union movement from Liberalism, and Keir Hardie, its leader, is rightly considered to be its real founder. The great service which he rendered was not in the realm of theory, but of practice. He had the prescience to see that a body of working men returned to Parliament, pledged to act with complete independence of either of the Capitalist parties, was bound in due course to adopt the Socialist faith. He, therefore, concentrated on the point of immediate practical importance, that of separating organised labour from dependence on Liberalism, and the creation of an independent Labour party in the country and in the House of Commons.

The inspiring force of the movement which made the Labour Party was the original I.L.P. This organisation, with its branches scattered widely throughout the country, carried on a ceaseless propaganda for Socialism, and for the conversion of the workers to the conception of independent political action. Its note was its inclusiveness. It did not preach doctrinaire Socialism but, using the tools provided for it by the Fabian Society, preached a practical doctrine on an ethical basis.

Year after year at the Trades Union Congress Hardie and others put forward their plea for independent political action. Meanwhile the great uprising of the unskilled workers which is best remembered from the great Dock Strike of 1889 had brought new life into the Trade Union movement. The most prominent leaders were members of the Social Democratic Federation, and it is perhaps in this field that the Federation did its greatest service to the British Socialist movement.

At last, in 1899, a motion was carried at the Trades Union Congress for the calling together of a conference of Trades Unions, Socialist societies, and the Co-operative movement for the formation of a Labour Representation Committee, and in 1900 this was created, with Mr. Ramsay MacDonald as secretary. The effective forces in the new organisation were the Trade Unions and the I.L.P., for the S.D.F. very quickly departed.

It is, perhaps, typical of this country that the event which resulted in the return of the tiny group of Keir Hardie, Crooks, Shackleton, and Henderson, and in 1906 of the first real Labour Party, was not the inspiration of a great leader, or some grave industrial crisis, but a judgment of the House of Lords which deprived the Trade Unions of the legal status which they had enjoyed for many years. The decision in the Taff Vale case spurred the unions to action in order to amend the law. Twenty-nine independent Labour members were returned to the House of Commons, and the Labour Party was born. The keen Labour man might well hang on his walls a portrait of Lord Halsbury alongside that of Keir Hardie.

The new Labour Party was formed on a very simple basis—that of the return of Labour members to Parliament. For all the years up to the end of the war this simple object sufficed. In 1917 as in 1906 its object is stated to be: "To organise and maintain in Parliament and the country a political Labour Party."

The conception of the Labour Party at that date is well expressed by Mr. Wardle in his presidential address in 1911:

From the very first, the ties which bound the Party together were of the loosest possible kind. It has steadily and, in my opinion, wisely always refused to be bound by any programme, to subscribe to any dogma, or to lay down any creed. Its strength has been its catholicity, its tolerance, its welcoming of all shades of political and even revolutionary thought, provided that its chief object, the unifying of the workers' political power, was not damaged or hindered thereby.

He goes on to describe its policy as that of using its separate and independent existence to secure for the workers the utmost that the exigencies of the moment would permit.

The Labour Party in the House of Commons found itself alongside a body of Trade Unionists, mainly miners, of about the same strength who were returned as members of the Liberal Party. They, too, came to Parliament with the same objectives as the members of the Labour Party—to seek to wring from the Capitalist Government some advantages for the men whom they represented. It might well have seemed that the difference between the two groups was only one of tactics, but the real distinction was the inclusion in the ranks of the Labour Party of a number of active Socialists who had behind them a great propaganda machine, the I.L.P., and a great body of enthusiastic supporters who had no doubts as to the goal at which they aimed, which was Socialism.

During the years prior to the Great War it was still an open question as to whether from these beginnings a powerful Socialist movement would emerge. There was the possibility that it might revert to the position of a mere wing of the Liberal Party. The strength of the urge towards a two-party system in this country is very great. The average elector wants to back a winner. A party which is not in the competition for the achievement of power is in a very weak position.

The decision was not effected by the brilliance of the action of the Parliamentary Party, although some striking successes were won, especially the legislative reversal of the Taff Vale judgment, but mainly by the work of the Socialist propagandists in the unions and in the country. Liberal Labourism sustained a mortal blow by the decision of the miners in 1910 to join the

Labour Party, and henceforth this group ceased to have any importance, and disappeared as its old members died. It had no roots in the country.

Meanwhile, in the field of municipal politics there was an unceasing attack on the older parties entrenched in the local councils. Wherever this attack became formidable, it was met by a coalition of Liberal and Conservative Capitalists, so that the old unity of the Left was superseded by a unity of the Right, based on class interest.

The pre-war Parliamentary Party consisted entirely of men of working-class parentage and predominantly of Trade Union officials. Although some middle-class men stood as candidates of the Labour Party in pre-war years, none was elected. It was not until 1922 that any person with the social background of the middle classes was elected a Labour member of Parliament. The Party was, in fact, predominantly the expression on the political field of the Trade Unions, and its members, with the exception of a few I.L.P. representatives, had spent all their working life in the industrial movement. It was a strictly working-class party without any theoretical nexus. The middle-class man or woman who wished to serve the cause of Labour was a member of the Fabian Society, the S.D.F., or the I.L.P. The number of these at that time was sufficiently small to make the action of anyone from the professional or business classes who embraced the cause of Labour an eccentricity.

The organisation of the Party reflected naturally its class composition. There were some million and a half Trade Unionists affiliated. There were a large number of Trades Councils and nearly eighty local Labour Parties. These were composed of local branches of Union and Socialist societies. Over large areas in the country the I.L.P. was the only local organisation in the Party.

The Labour Party was still primarily a Trade Union body. It was not as yet a serious competitor for power with the older parties. Its candidates, for whom in each case an affiliated organisation provided the financial backing, did not amount even to a hundred. The Labour Party, in effect, up to the end of the war was still only a section, with largely a sectional appeal.

THE WAR

The Great War was a turning-point in the history of the Labour Party. As with all Socialist Parties, the war revealed grave dissensions in its ranks between those who in face of the national emergency thought it right to stand in with their fellow countrymen even to the extent of taking office in a Capitalist Government, and those who considered it their duty to continue to oppose in every way a Government which was engaging in war. In the Labour Party the greater number of those who took the latter course did so from Christian pacifist convictions rather than from the class-war standpoint. It speaks much for the strength of the structure that had been erected that it was not shattered, and it is due to the temperament of the people of this country that, despite all the bitterness of the war years, and the deep cleavages of opinion that developed, the Labour Party preserved its unity and was ready to play its part as a united force in the new world which the peace brought.

It would be interesting to speculate on the course of British politics and the fortunes of the Labour Party if the war had not taken place, and to consider how far this event hastened the advent of a Socialist Party. In the political field the outstanding fact was the shattering of the Liberal Party, thus leaving the way clear for its successor. In the industrial field, the war and the immediate post-war years brought an immense increase of membership and a realisation of the importance of the workers which destroyed much of the previous acceptance of inferiority. In the realm of ideas the invasion of industry by the State, and the large-scale undertakings in planned organisation, lent a new weight to many of the contentions of Socialists and weakened the resistance to

HISTORICAL RETROSPECT

change. Above all, perhaps, the breaking-up of old habits of life made the average man and woman—for women now received the franchise—more receptive of new ideas.

The new era was marked by two big changes in the Labour Party. The first was organisational. The institution of individual membership and the consequent development of local Labour Parties enabled the Labour Party to appeal to wider sections of the community. It gave more weight to the constituency organisation than it had had before. The Party became organised fully on a territorial basis.

The second was ideological. The Party now adopted Socialism as its aim. No longer is the mere return of Labour members sufficient. In 1918 the objects of the Party were set out approximately as they stand to-day.

PARTY OBJECTS

NATIONAL

1. To organise and maintain in Parliament and in the country a Political Labour Party, and to ensure the establishment of a Constituency Labour Party in every County Constituency and every Parliamentary Borough, with suitable divisional organisation in the separate Constituencies of Divided Boroughs.

2. To co-operate with the General Council of the Trades Union Congress, or other Kindred Organisations, in joint political or other action in harmony with the Party Constitution and Standing Orders.

3. To give effect as far as may be practicable to the principles from time to time approved by the Party Conference.

4. To secure for the workers by hand or by brain the full fruits of their industry and the most equitable distribution thereof that may be possible, upon the basis of the common ownership of the means of production, distribution, and exchange, and the best obtainable system of popular administration and control of each industry or service.

5. Generally to promote the Political, Social, and Economic Emancipation of the People, and more particularly of those who depend directly upon their own exertions by hand or by brain for the means of life.

INTER-DOMINION

6. To co-operate with the Labour and Socialist organisations in the Dominions and the Dependencies with a view to promoting the purposes of the Party, and to take common action for the promotion of a higher standard of social and economic life for the working population of the respective countries.

INTERNATIONAL

7. To co-operate with the Labour and Socialist organisations in other countries and to assist in organising a Federation of Nations for the maintenance of Freedom and Peace, for the establishment of suitable

machinery for the adjustment and settlement of International disputes by Conciliation or Judicial Arbitration, and for such International Legislation as may be practicable.

PARTY PROGRAMME

1. The Party Conference shall decide from time to time what specific proposals of legislative, financial, or administrative reform shall be included in the Party Programme.

No proposal shall be included in the Party Programme unless it has been adopted by the Party Conference by a majority of not less than two-thirds of the votes recorded on a card vote.

2. The National Executive Committee and the Executive Committee of the Parliamentary Labour Party shall decide which items from the Party Programme shall be included in the Manifesto which shall be issued by the National Executive Committee prior to every General Election. The joint meeting of the two Executive Committees shall also define the attitude of the Party to the principal issues raised by the Election which are not covered by the Manifesto.

The adoption of this programme was followed by the issue of the first comprehensive statement of the policy of the Labour Party. Hitherto the Party had been guided in its action by the various resolutions passed at the annual conferences. A study of them will show very clearly the attitude of the Party. They are, apart from some very general resolutions, the expression of the aims of a minority group seeking limited reforms. There is no attempt to indicate priorities or to lay down any policy for a Party in the event of its attaining power. Indeed, such a prospect was too remote to be worth considering. The resolutions express that unity of all shades of Labour opinion which Mr. Wardle referred to in the address quoted above. To a party still in the propaganda stage there will be attracted all sorts and conditions of men and women who advocate unpopular or minority doctrines. Some may be really individualists, but they will work with a Socialist Party because of the need for minorities to seek mutual support. The Labour Party in its pioneer stage had no need to think out exactly the relationship to one another of the various proposals which it sponsored.

Labour and the New Social Order, which was the call of Labour to the men and women who had just come through a great war, was a remarkable document. It was very lengthy and diffuse, dealing with a great variety of subjects, including such matters as Home Rule for Ireland, married women's income tax, and temperance reform. Within it all Labour adherents could find their own particular reforms. It did not represent at all the attitude of mind of people who expected shortly to be called upon to administer the affairs of the country. It was a declaration of faith and aspirations rather than a political programme. It was, however, an uncompromisingly Socialist document. It stated that its proposals proceeded from definitely held principles, and went on to declare that Labour stood for a deliberately planned co-operation in production and distribution for the benefit of all who participate by hand or by brain. The manifesto was drawn up while the war was still in progress, and it is, therefore, natural that it should have been much concerned with the question as to how the nation was to return to a peace-time basis. It did not consider for a moment the re-establishment of pre-war Capitalist industry. The war, it stated, saw " the culmination and collapse of a distinctive industrial civilisation, which the workers will not seek to reconstruct." The war had seen a rapid extension of Government control over industry. Labour was anxious to retain the power of the community over those industries which were essential to the welfare of the nation.

Allowing, however, for the difference in the country's position in 1918 and to-day, the programme shows that as far as general principles are concerned Labour stood then where it stands to-day. For nine years *Labour and the New Social Order* remained the Party's official programme.

Parallel with this development of a programme went the organisation of the Party in the country.

The great influx into the unions during and immediately after the war swelled the number of Labour adherents. The formation of local Labour Parties with individual sections broadened its basis. The enfranchisement of women, which the Party had always strongly supported, gave rise to the formation of women's sections, and enlisted in the ranks very many of those who had given devoted service to the women's cause and had become trained speakers and organisers.

The extension of the franchise created a huge new electorate, including a far greater proportion of the youth of the nation. It put an end also to the small constituencies in which the electorate were open to the influence of tea-fights and charities. The Party was fortunate in having in its secretary, Arthur Henderson, a first-class organiser who created the most effective political machine in the country.

The notorious war election of 1918 found the Labour Party strengthened in numbers, but still considered as only a section of the Opposition. It was at that time still possible that there might be a Liberal revival. Labour was treated on an equality with the Liberals who were opposed to the Coalition. Its real strength was not so much in the House of Commons as in the country. There was in the ranks of the governing classes a very lively fear of revolution. The existence of large numbers of unemployed ex-servicemen who demonstrated with discipline as well as enthusiasm held dangerous possibilities. The Trade Unions were strong in numbers and full of militancy. Above all, the workers as a whole had been made to understand their importance. Behind all demands there loomed the menace of the general strike. The Triple Alliance of the Miners, Railwaymen, and Transport Workers was a powerful influence in inducing the Government to enact considerable measures of social reform, which were regarded as an insurance against revolution.

The election which marked the end of the war coalition increased the strength of the Party to nearly 150, and raised it to the position of being the official Opposition. For the first time the idea of a Labour Government appeared a possibility. The sudden appeal to the country of Mr. Baldwin in 1923 made it a fact.

THE FIRST LABOUR GOVERNMENT

Mr. Ramsay MacDonald, who had been raised to the leadership of the Party by the votes of the I.L.P., became the first Labour Prime Minister, with a Government depending for its day-to-day support upon one or other of the Capitalist parties. It was obvious that not very much could be accomplished under such conditions. The general line taken by the Government was that of demonstrating that it was possible for Labour men and women to administer the country. Undoubtedly this demonstration had its utility. The British elector is very sceptical of anything which he has not seen. The mere formation of a Labour Government and its existence for nine months registered a vital change in the political situation. Henceforth Labour was the alternative Government. On the other hand, a bolder policy might well have been more successful. The greatest success was scored in foreign affairs, of which I treat elsewhere. The reason for this was that only in this sphere had policy been clearly worked out. On the home front there had been no real decision as to what should be done first. Useful work was done, but nothing very striking.

The fall of the Government resulted from a General Election in which, although numbers of votes increased, the membership in the House was reduced. During the next five years the Party was in Opposition and the fight was taken up on the industrial field. The General Strike was tried and defeated, but, despite this set-back, the strength of the Party increased. In 1928 a new programme was drawn up to replace *Labour and the New Social Order*. The new document, *Labour and the Nation*, differed considerably from its predecessor in its line of approach. It reflected in the first place the changed position of the Party. It was a bid for power by a Party which expected in the normal course to attain it. It was for this reason more constructive. It was, however, a very long document, and, though not so all-embracing as its predecessor, comprised a bewildering number of subjects. A four-page summary set out no less than seventy-two proposals that a Labour Government, if elected, intended to carry out. It was obvious that nothing short of a miracle could have enabled the Party, even with an overwhelming majority, to get all these measures passed into law within the life of one Parliament, yet there was no suggestion as to which of them was to be given priority. It was, indeed, designed to rally to the Party a great variety of supporters. It gave the Prime Minister an opportunity to select which items suited him. It gave every malcontent unlimited opportunities of charging the Party with breaches of faith for not implementing all these promises.

Before dealing with the second Labour Government there are certain developments in the activities of the Party to be noticed. While the Party in Parliament was being slowly increased, great strides had been made in capturing local councils for Labour. The small beginnings of pre-war days had grown enormously. In 1919 sixteen of the Metropolitan Borough Councils fell to the Labour attack. In the provinces many great cities had Socialist majorities. In the mining areas of Durham, Glamorgan, and Monmouth the County Councils, long regarded as impregnable, went overwhelmingly Labour. Although there have been occasional set-backs, the progress made since the war has been continuous. Cities such as Glasgow, Leeds, and Sheffield and very many smaller ones have given the opportunity to Labour men and women to put their ideals into practice. The London County Council, which long resisted, has now fallen, and the victory won in 1933 was repeated in 1936. The effect on the Party has been twofold. It has, first of all, given a great many of its members invaluable experience, and has enabled them to give concrete illustration of what Labour in power can do. On the other hand, it has tended to lessen the propaganda activities of many of the ablest exponents of Socialism owing to their having become absorbed in local administration.

THE SECOND LABOUR GOVERNMENT

The General Election of 1929 found Labour for the first time the largest Party in the House of Commons, with 288 members. Against it was ranged the Conservative Party, with 267, while holding the balance was the Liberal Party, with 59 members, temporarily united under the leadership of Mr. Lloyd George. The Liberal Party had gone to the country on a programme of advanced social reform. It had polled over five million votes, which, together with Labour's eight and a half million, made some fourteen millions against a total of less than nine million votes cast for a Conservative policy. There was, therefore, a clear mandate from the country for a programme which would be generally to the Left.

On the other hand, the Liberal Party was a collection of persons of very different views, united, it has been said, by a common distrust of their leader.

There were, it seems to me, three possible courses open to the Labour Party: to refuse office, to accept office and invite defeat by putting forward a Socialist programme and placing the onus of rejecting it on to the Liberal Party, or to come to some agreement with the Liberals on a programme which would secure joint action in the House. The first was hardly practical politics at that time, and might well have meant another General Election, which the Party could not then have afforded, while it would have lost ground through what would have been held to be lack of courage and unwillingness to accept responsibility. The second, while open to the same danger of making probable another General Election, would have been a good fighting policy, and, in view of the economic trend of the period, have been the wisest tactics. The third offered considerable possibilities, but had its own disadvantages in the difficulty of securing at the same time support of the Simonite Liberals and of the Left

Wing of the Labour Party. United action on a bold and challenging programme might have given good results.

No one of these courses was followed. Mr. MacDonald was quite right in thinking that in the sphere of foreign affairs a great lead for peace and disarmament could be given, but he had no clear idea as to what course to follow in domestic affairs. He seemed to think that by a course of studious moderation he could conciliate opposition, while doing enough to retain the support of his own followers. He had for some years been more and more attracted by the social environment of the well-to-do classes. He had got more and more out of touch with the rank and file of the Party, while the adulation which is almost inseparable from the necessary publicity given to the leader of a great movement had gone to his head and increased his natural vanity. The philosophy of gradualness which he had always maintained became almost indistinguishable from Conservatism, while his innate disinclination to take the necessary executive decisions made him readily accept the impossibility of any serious challenge to the powers that be. Mr. Snowden, his chief lieutenant, had unfortunately a negative mind, which service at the Exchequer tended to confirm. The result was that those who wished for a vigorous lead in home affairs found themselves side-stepped and frustrated at every turn.

HISTORICAL RETROSPECT

The achievements of the Government were, however, considerable, and in the field of foreign affairs, thanks to Mr. Henderson, very great. It is possible that had the times been more normal the policy followed might have been successful, but the advent of the world economic crisis changed the situation. It was abundantly clear that no mere carrying on of things as they were would suffice. Drastic action was necessary. Mr. MacDonald, however, had fortified himself with an economic advisory council mainly drawn from upholders of the existing system, and their advice strengthened him in his determination to take no heroic action. He was greatly helped in preserving his position in the Party by the action of the Left Wing of the I.L.P., whose tactics frequently caused others who were discontented to rally to the support of the Government.

It is not possible to know at what stage in the period of office of the Labour Government Mr. MacDonald determined to betray those who had given him their trust. I think that he had had the idea for some time at the back of his mind, and that his plans were laid several months before the actual breach with the Party. There is little doubt that his vanity had caused him to over-estimate his influence with the Party, and that he imagined that he would get far greater support than he did.

It is unnecessary to relate at length here the course of events which resulted in the formation of the National Government, and shortly after in the General Election of 1931 and the reduction of the Labour Party in the House of Commons to a handful. The most notable fact was that so few members of the Party followed Mr. MacDonald in his betrayal. Apart from Mr. Snowden and Mr. Thomas, no leaders went with him. With the exception of Lords Sankey and Amulree and Sir William Jowitt, no one else of any consequence deserted the cause of Labour. No affiliated body, local or national, lent him its support. When one considers previous splits in political parties such as that caused by the Liberal Unionist secession or by the Lloyd George–Asquith controversies in the Liberal Party, the difference is striking. There was, in fact, no split, but only the shedding of a few leaves from the top of the tree, with a few parasitic appendages. The trunk and the main branches weathered the storm.

The effect, however, on the Party was profound. The shock at the betrayal of the cause by men like MacDonald and Snowden, who had done so much to further it in the past, was felt deeply by thousands of devoted members throughout the country, and their faith was severely shaken. The loss to Parliament of many of the ablest and most experienced members who were defeated at the polls put back the Party in the estimation of the general public. The Left Wing dissidents split in two; one part, the I.L.P., wrapped itself in self-righteous isolation, seeking to rid itself of any responsibility for the actions of the Labour Party while in office. On the other hand, Sir Oswald Mosley and a few associates formed a separate party, which soon developed into a Fascist organisation.

While the immediate shock was severe, the general effect on the Party was salutary. It led to a re-examination of its fundamental position. It caused a reaffirmation of its aims and objects. Mr. MacDonald had led the Party into an acceptance of gradualness and a frame of mind which tended to acquiesce in things as they are. The Party under his guidance laid too much stress on continuity and on the fundamental unity of society, to the neglect of its discordancies.

The increase in numbers in the House had been to a large extent due to the differences in the ranks of the Capitalists, which caused Labour men and women to think that more progress in the conversion of the electorate had been made than was actually the fact. In 1931 Capitalism closed its ranks and showed the real situation. The revulsion from MacDonaldism caused the Party to lean rather too far towards a catastrophic view of progress and to emphasise unduly the conditions of crisis which were being experienced, and to underestimate the recuperative powers of the Capitalist system.

In the years that followed, the small group in the House of Commons, under the very able leadership of George Lansbury, put up a great fight against heavy odds, while in the country the Labour Party gradually regained its strength and confidence.

One feature of MacDonaldism needs to be specially emphasised. The attempt was made to make people believe that there was really no need for the existence of separate parties, as all good men were working for a common end. MacDonaldism is, in fact, in its philosophy essentially Fascist. MacDonald himself uses the same phrases that may be found in the mouth of Hitler and Mussolini. He constantly draws a distinction between party and national interests, the theory being that there is really some ideal course to be followed for the good of the country and that party policies are deflections caused by mere factiousness. If MacDonald had succeeded in seducing any large proportion of the Labour Party, it is quite possible that the country might have swallowed this doctrine. The steadfastness of the rank and file of the Labour Party, in fact, saved British democracy.

I deal elsewhere with the controversies as to Socialist method which are now troubling the Party. They are the fruit, to a large extent, of difficulties in the sphere of foreign policy. I do not believe that they will result in anything like a serious split, because there is greater fundamental unity in the Party than ever before.

I have traced the Party from its small beginnings to its present position, where it is the alternative force in politics to Capitalism. More than ever to-day there stands out the difference between the two systems, Socialism and Capitalism. Liberalism as a coherent philosophy of politics is dead. What was of value in it has been taken over by Labour, and some part of its spirit has even gone towards modifying Conservatism.

CHAPTER III

TRADE UNION AND CO-OPERATIVE MOVEMENTS

I HAVE SHOWN that the Labour Party was the creation of the Trade Union movement, which joined with the Socialist movement to take action on the political field in order to supplement industrial action. The relationship between these two sides of the Labour movement requires to be examined more closely.

The Trade Union movement has two aspects. It is, in the first place, an organisation of the wage-earners working within the framework of Capitalist society in order to defend its members from injustice and to gain for them advantages. On the other hand, it is also an opposition to the existing system of society which it seeks to alter. It follows from this dual function that its methods of action must be such as to satisfy these two requirements. It cannot subordinate the immediate interests of its members entirely to the attainment of its ultimate aims or for purely political ends. On the other hand, it cannot sacrifice its ideals for society as a whole in order to obtain some transient advantages for a section of its membership, or even its entire membership. It must necessarily hold a balance. Its leaders owe a responsibility to the members who have joined their organisations for certain definite advantages. It is useless and harmful to look at the Trade Unions purely as a revolutionary force to be subservient to the demands of the political leaders. It is equally dangerous for the Trade Unions to regard the politicians merely as an agency for obtaining particular advantages for organised Labour.

I may illustrate this by considering two phases of the movement. There have been those who have considered that, in pursuance of the doctrines of the class war, there should never be a truce on the industrial field, and that any agreement with the enemy was tantamount to a betrayal of the cause of the workers. They have therefore set themselves against the constituted authorities of the Trade Unions. They have fomented unofficial strikes and minority movements. They have always been ready to call for strikes for political purposes; to demand, for instance, that the transport workers should take direct action to stop munitions going to a foreign Power which was oppressing the workers. The pursuit of such tactics is necessarily a great embarrassment to those who are responsible for the direction of the actions of great masses of men, and for the dispensing of the funds which have been subscribed by them. It is their business to survey the field as carefully as the general staff of an army. They must decide when and where to attack and when to hold the line. They must concentrate their attacks on the objectives which offer the best possibility of success. They cannot countenance an irregular, guerilla warfare. They are in the position of a responsible Government. When they have won a victory, they must consolidate it; and when they have established the rule of law in a certain part of the industrial world by coming to definite agreements, they must keep them or surrender to anarchy. Nothing has done so much to create hostility to the Communist Party as their underground activities on the industrial field.

On the other side there are suggestions from time to time which would tend to make the Trade Unions merely an adjunct to the present Capitalist system. In return for certain definite benefits they would enter into something like a partnership with the employers. The Mond–Turner conversations had, in my view, this tendency. Still more sinister are the approaches made from time to time to sections of the workers to join with the employers in using the position of a particular industry to extort concessions from the rest of the community regardless of the general interest. It would, for instance, be perfectly possible for a big monopoly, by conceding to its workers conditions above that of the general body of employees, to attempt to enlist them into its service so that they would become accessary to the exploitation of the community.

I have put this duality in rather an extreme form in order to bring it out more clearly. In actual fact it seldom emerges in such a crude way, but it does, nevertheless, exist.

There are Unions in which the everyday work is so much a matter of co-operation with the employers that their leaders tend to forget or ignore the ultimate aims of the movement. They have become so constitutional that they are in essence Conservative. There have been instances, on the other hand, of the capture of Unions by extremists, who have, by a policy of continual strife, ultimately ruined the organisation because they constantly exacted from the members sacrifices which should not have been demanded except on some major issue.

In the vast majority of instances the Trade Unions are successful in avoiding the dangers of either course. Without sacrificing their ultimate aim, and without allowing discipline to destroy enthusiasm, they obtain for their members security and status. On the other hand, the Labour Party, although it originated as a group of Trade Unionists sent to Parliament with the specific object of supporting organised Labour by action on the political field, is not a mere political expression of Trade Unionism. The Trade Unions are the backbone of the movement, but the Party represents something more than the needs of organised Labour. It is a national party with a Socialist objective. It must therefore, while being ready to support the demands of organised Labour, have due regard to the interests of all sections of the workers and of the nation as a whole. It may come to the conclusion that certain immediate demands of a Trade Union are in conflict with Socialist policy. It may find it necessary to emphasise the temporary character of some arrangement agreed to by the Unions. It is the partner, not the servant, of the Trades Union Congress. Similarly it has no right to expect the Trades Union Congress to do its work for it, or to take the burden of decisions which it ought to bear itself. In fact these difficulties seldom arise, because of the close contact between the two bodies; although when the Labour Party was in office relations were not always as good as they might have been—just because of lack of contact.

Trade Unions operate in a comparatively restricted sphere. They are concerned with the interests of their members as producers of goods and renderers of services. They are occupied with questions of wages, hours, and conditions of labour. There may be differences of opinion on tactics. There may be divergencies of interest between craft and craft, or even between the workers of one area and another, but there are no serious cross-currents which might cause division. The weapon of the Trade Unionist is solidarity. The success of a Union depends on getting all its members to take action simultaneously, and to observe strict loyalty. It follows that it is of the essence of Trade Unionism that the will of the majority must prevail. Once a decision has been arrived at, all must conform. Whatever may have been the difference of opinion among the members as to the wisdom of the decision, there is no room for individual action once the die is cast. Throughout all Trade Union activities this solidarity obtains. When the Executive of a Union or of the Trades Union Congress comes to a conclusion, all the members, whatever their previous opinions, support it.

No such absolute solidarity is attainable in a political party. The questions with which the politician has to deal embrace the whole range of human activity—political, religious, economic, and cultural. He has to give expression to the views of his constituents, not merely as producers of wealth, but as consumers and also as citizens. He represents the women in the home as well as the workers. He represents localities as well as occupations. The Parliamentary Labour Party is therefore necessarily exposed to more cross-currents of opinion than is the Trades Union Congress.

To take an obvious instance. A Bill may be introduced dealing with education. The Party will either approve or disapprove of its main provisions. It may be, on the whole, a useful measure from the general standpoint of the interests of the workers, but there may also be particular interests. Some members may belong to a particular religious denomination or represent electors holding strongly a special point of view. The elected member has to bear in mind his general loyalty to the Party, and also his obligations to those whom he represents. Again, a Bill may be introduced which specially affects a particular area or some one industry. It may be advantageous from the point of view of the immediate interests of a section of organised Labour, but may at the same time embody principles fraught with danger if generally applied. In all these cases there must be a balance struck and careful consideration given before a decision is taken.

Again, on matters of foreign policy questions arise which affect the deep religious convictions of some members who differ from the majority. In such cases the Party wisely gives a good deal of latitude. The point I desire to make is: that the questions which have to be faced in Parliament are often complex, and that it is quite impossible to force on members a rigid discipline without risking serious trouble. This difficulty is not peculiar to the Labour Party. It is found in all political movements except those which are content to surrender all free will to the dictatorship of an autocrat or a caucus. It is, nevertheless, very rare for any serious difficulty to arise between the political and the industrial wings of the movement.

This difference of function, then, has to be borne in mind by both the industrial and political sides of the movement if they are to work harmoniously together. There is also necessarily a certain difference of outlook in the members of the three executive bodies in the Labour movement. The T.U.C. consists, for the most part, of general secretaries of Unions who are engaged in the heavy day-to-day work of administration. There is, therefore, to a large extent, a common attitude among the members, due to identity of occupation. The Labour Party Executive, on the other hand, while it contains a number of Trade Union officials, has a more varied membership. It brings together the administrator, the politician, and the propagandist. The Parliamentary Labour Party Executive, while not dissimilar in composition to that of the Labour Party, consists of representatives who necessarily have their outlook conditioned by the parliamentary background. They do their work in the peculiar conditions of the constant struggle with their opponents on the floor of the House. They meet their immediate constituents, the members of the Parliamentary Party, week by week, and decide with them on policy. In matters of joint concern to the three bodies the T.U.C. has more power of decision than is entrusted to the Executive of the Parliamentary Labour Party. The latter, to put it shortly, cannot deliver the goods to the same degree as the former.

This distinction is of great importance when it comes to a question of joint action between the three bodies, in matters in which they are all concerned, and may be a cause of friction.

There is yet another distinction to be borne in mind, and that is the conditions under which they have to do their work.

Trade Union representatives, in dealing with employers, have, of course, to deal with immediate issues and also matters of long-term policy. They have to intervene in a dispute. They have to meet the employers, get the best terms they can, and persuade their members to accept or reject terms, but in all these cases they have the opportunity of consulting with each other and with their members apart from their opponents. In the political battle in the House of Commons the fight has to be carried on in the open. The leader must give a lead to his followers who are there behind him actually engaging with the enemy. The kind of discipline and leadership possible under these conditions is something quite different from that which obtains in the industrial field.

The fight in Parliament has its own technique, which cannot be very easily understood by those who have not experienced it.

It is therefore inevitable that there should from time to time be misunderstandings between the industrial and the political sides of the movement. The Trade Union leaders do not always understand the exigencies of political warfare, but equally there is sometimes a lack of understanding on the part of Parliamentarians of the necessary conditions of Trade Union action. They are apt to consider that Trade Union leaders have more power than is actually the case. For instance, when the first Labour Government was in office there were a number of industrial disputes which embarrassed it. There were those among the political leaders of Labour who seemed to think that by a word the Trade Union leaders could have stopped industrial action. They were quite wrong. The Trade Union leader, like the political leader, has only a certain amount of power. He derives it from his supporters, and he cannot flout their wishes.

The attitude of the opponents of Labour towards Trade Union influence on the Labour Party is interesting and amusing. The Labour

Party is sometimes described as being entirely in the hands of Trade Union "bosses." Its leaders are depicted as going, cap in hand, to get their orders from their taskmasters and paymasters. It is said to be deplorable that a political party should be completely dominated by the "narrow-minded autocrats" of the Unions. At other times a contrast is drawn between the true and patriotic Trade Union leaders and the factious Socialist politicians. The former are then described as men of judgment and responsibility, while the latter are, at best, woolly idealists, and, at the worst, the tools of foreigners and revolutionary intriguers.

The attitude adopted, of course, depends on the position at the moment. The truth about the relationship between the political and industrial sides is really very simple. There is no attempt by either side to "boss" the other. There is a recognition of their partnership in action on behalf of the workers, and of their freedom of action in their respective spheres.

In order to bring about the greatest amount of co-operation there has been created the National Council of Labour, on which sit representatives of the T.U.C., the Labour Party Executive, and the Parliamentary Party. The work of this body is essentially co-ordinating and not mandatory. It is not a super-authority with the right to enforce its decisions on its constituent bodies. The most it can do is to recommend. The industrial and the political sides keep each other informed of their respective activities, but there is no intrusion into one another's sphere. Where joint action is necessary, it is concerted. On occasions there are meetings of all three executives—especially recently, on grave questions of foreign policy. The resulting unity of action is not obtained by enforcing the views of one body on the others, but by evolving, through agreement, a common line of policy.

It might be thought that as the Labour Party is composed predominantly of representatives of the Trade Unions, and as the Labour Party Conference is representative of the Unions which control a majority of the votes, there should be no need for such consultation. It might be, and, indeed, sometimes is, thought that Trade Union opinion must be dominant throughout. This is to ignore the effect on the mind of a man of the sphere in which he is operating. Men are necessarily influenced in their attitude by the particular function which they are engaged in performing. They are not rigidly set by certain preconceptions. The same man in his capacity as a Trade Union official may take a slightly different attitude from that which he does as member of the Party Executive or as Member of Parliament. The considerations which are in his mind are naturally different, and the conclusions at which he arrives are influenced by his association with others. If this were not so, these would be little good in consultation.

Close co-operation between the two sides of the movement becomes ever more important as the attainment of power comes nearer. It was one of the great errors of Mr. MacDonald that he failed, when Prime Minister, to maintain the contact which was necessary with the Trade Unions. Each side must influence the other. The political side has to bear in mind that Socialism is not just State Capitalism. The taking over of an industry by the State is not an end in itself—it is a means of attaining freedom. That implies a change in the status of the worker. He is in the future to be a citizen in his industrial as well as in his political capacity. A Labour Minister must never allow himself to forget the importance of this side of the changes which Socialism is going to effect. Equally important is it for the Trade Unionist to realise that the Union will be changing from an antagonistic to a co-operative position in industry when Socialism comes.

THE LABOUR PARTY AND THE CO-OPERATIVE MOVEMENT

The relationship between the Labour Party and the great organisations of consumers which form the Co-operative movement is less close than with the Trade Unions. All three movements start from the same fundamental position. All seek to substitute a new organisation of society based on service and labour instead of private profit and property, but their methods of action and their spheres of operation differ. The Co-operative movement, after its early days of experiment, settled down for the most part into a sustained attempt to substitute, as far as possible, for individualist profit-making a system of trading based on mutuality and sustained by the device of the dividend on purchases. On the productive side, while there is a considerable amount of productive co-operation on the Owenite model, the principal development has been in effect a form of " capitalism " wherein the producers receive wages from the organised consumers who take the place of the capitalist.

For many years the Co-operative movement eschewed politics, and there is even to-day a considerable hostility to political action by Co-operative Societies on the part of sections of the membership. It is, indeed, doubtful if the movement would have entered the political field at all but for the constant attacks made upon it, both by the multiple shops and the organisations of small traders, in Parliament. These have been indefatigable in their efforts to obtain legislation which would act as a check on their trade rivals. They only succeeded, however, when the country had been deluded into returning a "National" Government.

It was not till the end of the war that the Co-operative Party started, although units of the movement had often helped locally, and, both by taking part in demonstrations, and especially by rendering great service in industrial disputes, had shown its solidarity with the workers. It was not till 1918 that a Co-operative member was returned to the House of Commons. Since then the number of members has steadily increased.

The Co-operative members stand as members of the Co-operative Party, but in alliance with the Labour Party. So far as work in the House of Commons is concerned, there has never been any difficulty at all. Co-operative and Labour Party members work together as a team, and are, in effect, indistinguishable.

In the field of organisation there have been difficulties which are now being overcome. The exact relationship between two national parties was necessarily difficult of adjustment. Organisation questions, concerning methods of selection, financial assistance, and the status of agents, offer points on which differences have occurred.

As to policy, a very great degree of agreement has been attained. Of course such agreement is far easier in opposition to a Capitalist Government than when a Labour Government is in power. It is in the practical details of economic reconstruction that difficulties are likely to occur. An obvious instance was in connection with the marketing schemes of the Labour Government, which, in fact, imposed a form of State co-operation upon farmers in exchange for certain benefits. There was here the possibility of estrangement through the establishment of a form of distributive organisation rivalling that of the Co-operative Society. Goodwill and common sense, however, prevented any breach.

In another field of policy there has been, again, a possibility of rivalry. Enthusiasts for municipal trading advanced claims which seemed to come in conflict with the established interests of Co-operative Societies. The municipal administrator claimed that as, through the agency of the Council, the people were supplied with water and electricity, so they should be supplied with milk and bread and other necessities of life. The keen co-operator was apt to claim the whole field. Here, again, discussion has brought the two parties closer together. Both sides are realising that there is nothing sacrosanct about either forms of consumers' organisation. It is not a matter of principle at all, but one of convenience. Broadly speaking, the line of demarcation would seem to be that, where the commodity is in universal demand, and is of undifferentiated quality, it is generally better that it should be supplied by a State or municipal agency, but, where the element of choice enters in, the Co-operative Society gives the consumer greater freedom.

Larger questions will arise in the future. A Labour Government which is organising the food supplies of the nation will have to deal with imports. This might be done either by a State department or through the Co-operative Wholesale Societies, which already are responsible for a very great proportion of staple foods, or, again, by some combination of the two. The Co-operative movement is anxious that, in the event of a defeat of a Labour Government, its position should not be prejudiced. At the same time, it is willing to work in co-operation with a State agency on lines which would preserve its integrity.

Here there arises a difficulty somewhat similar to that which was noted in the case of the Trade Unions. The question is, can the Co-operative movement afford to combine whole-heartedly with a Labour Government in creating the new social order? Will it not be in danger, in the event of a defeat at the next General Election, of falling a prey to the vengeance of the Capitalists?

The other side to this is the question, can the Co-operative movement afford to stay out of a general reconstruction? If it does, may it not find itself restricted or even superseded?

These questions must be faced by those Co-operators who still think that it is possible to be neutral in the political struggle. They can have no illusions as to the attitude of private business towards them. A study of what has happened in Italy and Germany shows how a great movement can be liquidated and destroyed in Corporate States, and how short is the shrift that it will receive from its enemies.

There is, finally, one thing which must be recognised. The Co-operator necessarily looks at things from the point of view of the consumer. *Qua* consumer he wants things cheap. The same man in his capacity of producer wants high wages. There is here a possibility of dissension unless the two organisations which represent the workers in their two separate capacities work in close harmony. Differences to-day between Co-operative Societies and the National Union of Distributive and Allied Workers are worked out generally harmoniously, but this difference of outlook may show itself in the political field. Sections of the workers may be influenced, by their economic conditions, to favour tariffs, whilst the Co-operator is naturally a free trader. It is just here that the Labour Party provides a nexus between the two movements, and the cordial relations in the House of Commons between Labour men and Co-operators have shown the value of this. Moreover, the Trade

Union movement is predominantly representative of men's interests, though not so much as formerly, while the Co-operative movement is an expression of the interests of the woman in the home. The Labour Party, in its organisation and sphere of action, represents both of them.

In my view, it is of vital importance that the Co-operative movement should march in step with the Labour Party and the Trade Union movement. Full consultation beforehand, not merely on general principles, but on concrete proposals in the Labour programme, will eliminate difficulties. I am myself convinced that in the Socialist State of the future the organisation of the consumers must play a vital part. It is very noteworthy how in Russia, although starting out with very different ideas of the utility of the movement, the Government of the U.S.S.R. has found it vital to develop Co-operative organisation as an integral part of the economic structure. A real, living Co-operative movement is of first-class importance in order to give the consumer the opportunity of voicing effectively his demand. The Trade Unions, rightly, will carry great weight in saying under what conditions things shall be made, transported, and distributed, but it is the Co-operative movement, collectively and through the combined action of its membership as expressed in their purchases, which will largely determine what is to be produced. Recently an invitation was given to the Co-operative movement to be represented on the National Council of Labour. I hope that in due time this will be accepted, thus making this body the means of joint consultation for the whole movement.

The Co-operative Party has done a great service in bringing home to its members the importance of political action, and in keeping before them the ideals of the movement. All organisations of great size are liable to the seduction of their own machine. The Labour Party is in danger of thinking in terms of votes and constituency organisation, or perhaps of seats won. The Trade Union movement is in danger of thinking in terms of immediate benefits. The Co-operative movement is in danger of thinking of the dividend and material achievements. Success makes this danger all the greater. It can only be met by enthusiastic devotion to the ideals which are common to all three, and which can alone be achieved through their united action. It is the idealists who work within the movement who are most important. There are always outsiders who are prepared, for the sake of the ideal, to criticise the practical workers. Concentrating on criticism, their output of productive work is small. Sometimes they are so full of ideals that they cease to understand the practical things of everyday life. Sometimes they are such superior persons that they forget what the ordinary man is like. The strength of the Labour movement will be enhanced by a frank recognition of the different functions of its various organisations, and by a ready spirit of mutual understanding.

THE LABOUR PARTY AND THE INTERNATIONAL

The Labour Party forms part of the Labour and Socialist International, which is in line of succession of the old Second International, and is supported by most of the democratic parties in Europe and by some in other continents. Unlike the Third International, which is the creation of the Communists of Soviet Russia and is dominated by them, the L.S.I. cannot give orders to its affiliated organisations. It makes recommendations which are applied in each country in accordance with the circumstances existing there. It takes decisions on policy which are binding on those parties which agree to them. The full body meets from time to time as required, and the Bureau, which has its office in Brussels, at regular intervals. There are fourteen members of the Bureau, which acts as an Executive when the full body is not in session. The L.S.I. is, therefore, a consultative body for arranging joint action and correlating policy rather than a super-authority over the national parties. The progress of Fascism in Europe has seriously weakened the L.S.I., especially through the destruction of the great and powerful German Social Democratic Party which had for many years played a big part in its deliberations. The different conditions existing in the principal countries have made action on identical lines practically impossible. A further cause of weakness has been the creation of the Third International and the internecine strife thereby engendered. The L.S.I. plays, however, a very important part in maintaining the unity of the Socialist movements all over the world. The Bureau issues regular bulletins, which keep the constituent parties aware of one another's activities. Very large sums of money have been raised and disbursed in aid of the victims of tyranny, while in many instances the provision of legal assistance and the mobilisation of world public opinion have prevented judicial murders. The Matteotti Fund was created for this purpose. The L.S.I. keeps in close contact with the International Federation of Trades Unions, and on occasions joint meetings of the two bodies have been held. In the years 1936 and 1937 the two bodies co-operated in helping the Spanish Socialists in their struggle for liberty and democracy. Large sums of money were collected and supplies sent. The work of sending help to the Spanish people, in the form of food and clothing, was undertaken on a considerable scale, although for obvious reasons, in view of the blockade, it was impossible to advertise these activities. The two bodies decided, while maintaining the right of the Spanish Government to obtain arms and munitions, to acquiesce in the policy of nonintervention provided that it was worked fairly and made effective. The L.S.I., collectively and through its constituent parties, constantly endeavoured to bring pressure to bear to get this policy carried into effect.

In addition to its more formal activities the L.S.I. provides an opportunity for leading Socialists in many countries to make the personal contacts which are essential to mutual understanding.

CHAPTER IV

CONSTITUTION

THE CONSTITUTION of the Labour Party is inevitably the result of its history and expresses the balance of the various forces which have created it. Some Socialist movements have been from the outset the creation of an individual whose powerful personality has moulded the party into its particular form. Others have been created by a group of persons who, having the end clearly in mind, devised the means. The Labour Party, on the other hand, was, as I have shown, a structure erected on an existing foundation, the industrial movement of Trade Unionism. That foundation was essentially federal. Most of the great Unions to-day are the result of a very slow process of amalgamating groups of workers combined on a craft basis. In many instances, as, for example, in the Lancashire textile industry, the division by craft was supplemented by the division of locality.

Sidney and Beatrice Webb, in their classical works on Trade Unionism and Industrial Democracy, have traced the process whereby the small detachments of Trade Unionism were welded into regiments and the regiments into armies. The process took years of struggle against local and craft particularism. The young member of the Labour movement of to-day, looking at the impressive figures of membership of the great Trade Unions, is apt to disregard the history of their emergence and to underrate the individualistic forces that had to be overcome. Yet it is essential to remember this past history if one wishes to understand the constitution of the Labour Party.

The Labour Party is itself federal in constitution and is the child of a federal organisation— the Trades Union Congress. It shows in its structure the hereditary characteristics of the parent body. The natural basis for a political party in a country enjoying a constitution framed on the principles of representative democracy is the individual member. The geographical division of the country into constituencies provides a framework for the organisation of local parties. The result is a simple and logical structure.

The Labour Party, however, was not built on individual membership. It was originally designed to be the political expression of the Trade Union movement. Its units were not individuals, or even constituency parties, but affiliated societies. Its model was the Trades Union

Congress. Just as the Trades Union Congress is a federation for certain purposes of a number of independent societies, so the Labour Party, in its early years, was a federation for political purposes of certain Trade Unions and Socialist societies. The only way to become a member of the Labour Party was to join an affiliated society. It was only after 1918 that the doors were opened more widely and provision made for the enrolment of the individual member. The result of this historical development has been to make the constitution very complicated.

The Labour Party to-day comprises organisations of three main types. There are, first of all, the Trade Unions. These are affiliated nationally in respect of all those members who have signed a form contracting to pay the political levy. There are, secondly, Socialist societies, and, thirdly, constituency organisations. There is also one Co-operative Society nationally affiliated.

The constituency organisation, the divisional Labour Party, is itself composed of the local branches of Trade Unions and of Socialist and Co-operative Societies in its area which are affiliated to it, together with the individual members' section, comprising all those who join as individuals and who may or may not also be members through the affiliation of any other society to which they belong.

The Divisional Labour Party may also, in

county divisions, comprise a number of local Labour Parties. There will, too, in many instances, be a women's section, and a branch of the League of Youth, which is a special organisation for young people under twenty-one.

It will be seen that there is a considerable duplication of membership. A member of the Royal Arsenal Co-operative Society may be also a Trade Unionist, a member of the Fabian Society, and an individual member of the Divisional Labour Party, being thus a member four times over, and paying contributions four times through different bodies. At an Annual Conference his vote will be counted four times as a unit cast by the delegates of the various bodies of which he is a member. The total number of members in the Labour Party is nearly two and a half million, but a considerable deduction must be made for this duplication or even triplication of membership. Nearly two million of this total represent the affiliated membership of the Trade Unions, the remainder being divided between the other sections, of which by far the largest is that of individual members. In considering the working of the constitution it will be convenient to work up from the smaller units to the National Executive.

THE DIVISIONAL LABOUR PARTY

Throughout the whole of the constitution of the Labour Party the democratic principle is observed, and the greatest possible autonomy is given to the smaller units. The Divisional Labour Party is a microcosm of the whole organisation. It is composed of all the individual members in the area, and the members of the local branches of Trade Unions and Socialist societies that are affiliated to it. It is governed by a management committee composed of delegates of the affiliated organisations which are entitled to representation in accordance with their membership. The exact constitution varies somewhat from constituency to constituency. The Divisional Labour Party is a self-contained unit. It collects subscriptions from its members, paying a proportion to head office for its affiliation, and disposes of the remainder as it may decide. It chooses, subject to the approval of the National Executive, its own candidate for Parliament. It is entitled to one delegate to Conference for every thousand members upon which it pays fees, and an additional delegate for any part of a thousand. Within the Divisional Party there may be a number of local parties in the towns and villages in the constituency. These, again, may have a measure of autonomy in the selection of candidates for local authorities. Similarly, in urban areas, ward committees will be given delegated powers. The Divisional Party itself may form part of a Borough Labour Party or of a County Federation. These larger units are directly represented at the Annual Party Conference.

SOCIALIST SOCIETIES

For many years the Independent Labour Party was by far the most important Socialist society affiliated to the Labour Party. Its eight or nine hundred local branches were frequently the only live political force in their areas. Its influence lay not in its numbers, but in the intensity of the work done and in its political consciousness. The development of local Labour Parties with individual membership sections tended to supplant it in most areas, while the conversion of the rank and file of the movement to its principles led to its taking a critical rather than a constructive attitude. Eventually it decided to break with the Labour Party, losing in the process much of its membership. Its disaffection took away from the Party a valuable agency of propaganda which in some areas has not been replaced.

The Socialist League, which was formed to a large extent from former members of the I.L.P., for some time fulfilled the function of an energising and propaganda body, but later fell into the same error as did the I.L.P. It failed to realise that the advantages of affiliation to a larger body necessarily implied loyalty to its decisions. Its short and rather chequered career was ended in the summer of 1937.

The other Socialist societies either cater for special sections, such as professional or university members, or confine themselves to a particular kind of work, as does the Fabian Society. The Social Democratic Federation carries on an old tradition with loyal acceptance of the conditions of membership of the larger unit. Of recent years the University Labour Federation has built up a strong movement among undergraduates, especially at Oxford and Cambridge, where the Labour clubs are the strongest political organisations. The Party has hitherto wisely allowed them a good deal of latitude, recognising that youths cannot be rigidly restricted in their relations with those who hold other shades of political opinion.

THE TRADE UNIONS

The Trade Unions provide the Party with the bulk of its membership and of its central finance. The extent to which the members take an active part in political work, and the method whereby their delegations to the Annual Conference are selected and mandated, varies from union to union. I shall discuss their position later.

THE ANNUAL CONFERENCE

The final authority of the Labour Party is the Party Conference, held once a year regularly and on occasions more frequently. It is composed of the delegates of affiliated organisations which are entitled to be represented and to vote in accordance with the number of members upon whose behalf affiliation fees have been paid.

It is necessary here to say something of the finance of the Party. In a movement which is essentially working class there is no room for secret party funds built up by contributions from wealthy individuals in exchange for benefits received or expected. The Labour Party depends on pennies not pounds. The contributions paid by members to their organisations vary, but the amount sent to head office is the same for every member, and stands to-day at fourpence a year. This payment determines both representation and voting power. It is not the payment of higher contributions by the Unions that gives them the controlling power at the Annual Conference but the aggregation of a great number of members. The method whereby this is effected differs not at all from that which is applicable to Divisional Labour Parties. In both cases the delegates' vote is cast by virtue of the payments of a number of members. In both cases the vote cast may represent the views of some and misrepresent the views of others.

In contradistinction to Conservative conferences which simply pass resolutions that may or may not be acted upon, the Labour Party Conference lays down the policy of the Party, and issues instructions which must be carried out by the Executive, the affiliated organisations, and its representatives in Parliament and on local authorities. Conservative conferences are generally more like demonstrations than conferences. Leaders come down and make speeches, but they do not really depend on these gatherings to lay down lines of policy; far less do they in any way feel bound to follow them.

The Labour Party Conference is in fact a parliament of the movement. It is more; it is a constituent assembly, because it has the power of altering its own constitution.

At the earlier Conferences the Trade Unions predominated far more than they do to-day. Trades Councils and local Labour Parties were then less numerous and influential. Socialist societies took a very prominent part in their proceedings, but their strength was qualitative rather than quantitative and depended for its effect on the existence of sympathetic delegates among the Trade Unions. The broadening of the basis of the Party in 1918, admitting individual members, has altered in some degree the balance of the Conference. Trades Councils have dropped out, local Labour Parties have increased. The political unit, the Constituency Party, in many cases now represented in Parliament, has become of greater importance than in early pioneer days.

The business of Conference is always in excess of what can be accomplished in the time, but its character has also changed. Where formerly there were a number of debates on widely separated subjects, the tendency is now for the greater part of the time to be devoted to considering large issues of major policy embodied in policy documents put forward by the Executive.

The extent to which delegates come to Conference closely bound by instructions varies. Some local Parties go meticulously through every item of the agenda and give exact orders to their delegates, whilst others give a free hand on many matters. It might be thought that this instruction of delegates meant that speeches and discussion would be ineffectual, the issues having been decided previously. This happens no doubt on some subjects, but generally speaking the circulated agenda becomes transformed in the course of business by consultations between groups in order to obtain support for essentials rather than wording, so that the delegate may find that in the result he has to interpret his instructions, and the light in which he interprets them is that of the discussion. Frequently, too, the issues which emerge at a Conference arise out of the Annual Report or from some circumstance which was not envisaged at the time of the instruction of the delegates. There is, therefore, an opportunity for the Conference to be swayed by argument, and in practice this often occurs.

There is also an Annual Conference of Labour Women, composed of delegates from Trade Unions and women's sections and Socialist societies, which, while not neglecting general subjects, naturally concentrates on those of particular interest to women.

THE EXECUTIVE

The Conference elects an Executive which holds office for one year. It is responsible for carrying out the decisions arrived at, for interpreting policy, and for making decisions between Conferences. It also carries on the general administration of the Party. The Executive reflects the composite character of the movement. There are twenty-two elected members divided into four sections, each of which forms a separate constituency, in accordance with the organisations which nominate the candidates for office. Twelve are assigned to the Trade Unions, six to the local Labour Parties and one to the Socialist societies, Co-operative Societies, and professional organisations. There are also four seats for women, the candidates for which may be nominated by any organisation. For purposes of voting the delegates form a single electoral college. Votes may be cast by any section for all of the seats to be filled. Delegates cast the block votes to which their organisations are entitled.

It is here that a grievance of considerable substance arises. A combination of a number of big Unions can, if it so chooses, decide the composition of the entire Executive. Without the support of some of them no one can hope to be elected a member of the Executive. The smaller sections maintain that, therefore, the members elected to fill the seats in their sections do not represent the desires of the delegates in those sections. It is impossible to deny the justice of this claim. I think that it is certain that not infrequently the candidate who secures a majority of the votes of the local Labour Parties is not elected. It is unnecessary to allege that this is done of set purpose or as the result of bargaining, though the possibility of this cannot be excluded. It is a natural consequence of the method adopted. The claim has been often preferred that the representatives of each section should be elected by the votes of those in that section only. It is objected that such a course would be likely to cause sectionalism in the Executive itself. Two further complaints are made: one that the representatives of the smaller sections owing their seats to the favour of those who control the big block votes are likely to be unduly subservient to the Unions or to their officials; the other that the representation of the Unions on the Executive is secured by a species of bargaining for mutual support which has resulted at times in the election of Executive members whose attainments and position in the movement are not such as to make them useful members of a body which has to perform important functions.

I think that there is some ground for these complaints, but there are objections to the adoption of other methods of election. To allow the voting to be by the delegates without any weightage for membership would tend to cause an increase in the number of delegates which might make the Conference, already unwieldy, too big for effective work. Or, if the Conference were not increased, it might put a premium on flashy oratory and hysterical appeal as against more solid qualities. The Labour Party has had some unfortunate experiences of people whose histrionic abilities were out of all proportion to their other qualities, and it cannot be blamed for caution.

I think that it is probable that these difficult questions will be solved by some form of compromise which will strengthen the Executive without exposing it to the risks indicated above. The question of altering the Constitution in this respect is under active consideration by the

Executive, and is likely to be dealt with and settled by the next Party Conference.

THE WORK OF THE EXECUTIVE

The twenty-two elected members and the Leader of the Party, the Secretary and the Treasurer, who are members *ex officio*, carry on the routine work of the Party. Much of the work is done by standing sub-committees, such as the Finance and General Purposes, Organisation and Policy Committees. Questions of policy are dealt with by a range of policy sub-committees dealing with Finance and Trade, Constitutional questions, the Reorganisation of Industry, Local Government, Agriculture, and other subjects.

These committees co-opt prominent members of the Party with specialist knowledge, and investigate matters of policy and report to the Executive on the particular aspects of the Party's work with which they are concerned. There are also numerous joint committees with the Trades Union Congress for the discussion of subjects in which there is a common interest.

Under the Executive work the officials at head office and the organisers in the nine areas throughout the country, together with the Divisional Party secretaries. The work of the Executive is hampered to a degree not always realised even inside the movement by the paucity of its financial resources. Its income from affiliation fees is somewhere between forty and fifty thousand pounds a year (the Labour Party, unlike other Parties, always publishes its accounts in full), which works out at an average of eighty pounds for each parliamentary division. With this sum it has to pay for a large office and a staff of around sixty or seventy, to arrange for conferences and speakers throughout the country, to prepare the Party's literature, and to give grants to divisions which are in a bad way financially. It would, indeed, be impossible to carry on the Party's business were it not for the extraordinary amount of voluntary help that is received. Some divisions are able to afford a full-time agent whilst others depend entirely on voluntary service. In both cases the thing which counts is the voluntary work of the members.

It is here that the great difference between the Labour Party and the old political parties lies. There are of course in both the Conservative and Liberal Parties enthusiasts who give voluntary service, but it is small compared to that given in the Labour movement. There are thousands of men and women who devote all their spare time to the movement. They will lend their scanty house room for office work or committee rooms at election time. They will take their part in the more stimulating work of speaking at meetings, but they will also do the dull slogging work of envelope addressing, canvassing, carrying the platform, selling literature, and collecting subscriptions. They do it week in and week out and year after year without reward. They are the people who compose the real strength of the movement. Often they suffer for the cause. They are victimised (sometimes in the past they were assaulted); often they wear out their strength in the service of the faith in which they believe.

The local activities of the Labour Party are a practical school of democracy. The man or woman learns there how to work with others; he learns, or should learn, tolerance; he learns to keep his enthusiasm while accepting the limitations of the medium in which he works. Much of his time may be taken up in disheartening and tiresome endeavours to persuade his fellows to take the line which seems to him right. Much, again, may be wasted in adjusting personal differences or in discussing non-essentials, but all this is an integral part of political training in a democracy. Those who have not experienced the drudgery of the everyday work of the movement in its local aspects have lost something which they cannot get in any other way.

I have now given a general sketch of the constitution of the Labour Party and have pointed out that it is something which is the result of historical growth rather than of logical planning. Undoubtedly, if a fresh start were to be made a simpler structure would be built up, but the difficulty of introducing any change now is very great.

The most common objection taken is that the Party is dominated by the Trade Unions, who, by the power of the block vote, determine all major issues. It is further suggested that the decision is not so much that of the rank and file of the Trade Unions as of the general secretaries and other officials. I discuss elsewhere the general relations between the Labour Party and the T.U.C. Here it is enough to say that, while there is undoubtedly some ground for complaint, it is very doubtful whether there would be any substantial change in the character of the decisions made if the block vote were removed.

Every vote by a delegate means that some minority is misrepresented. A Trade Union representative casting a vote for 50,000 members may have 30,000 on one side and 20,000 on the other, but, similarly, 50 local Labour Parties casting 1,000 votes each may all of them include minorities which are misrepresented. It is indeed a necessary feature of democracy that the minority should acquiesce in the decisions of the majority.

Even if the Party were made up solely of local Labour Parties, there would be differences of voting strength among them, and there would still be the possibility of complaint. It might be alleged that certain areas with small memberships found their interests neglected and their resolutions steam-rollered by the votes of the stronger and better organised districts.

The real difficulty is one which is a necessary incident in any large organisation. A delegate comes to an Annual Conference either fully instructed or with general directions; the agenda is always crowded and complicated, and the issues that arise are not infrequently those on which no definite instructions have been given. Sometimes the crucial vote may be given, not on a substantive motion, but on a resolution back or a motion for next business. It is here that the delegates wielding a large voting power have the pull. On many occasions this power will be fairly exercised, although there may be a certain tendency towards a conservative attitude. One must set against this, on the other hand, the danger of a conference being stampeded into unwise and precipitate action. I think on the whole it will be found that Trade Union leaders do not exercise their power tyrannically.

In fact, the main objection is generally found to be less against the method of voting than against the results of the voting. Those who make the loudest song about the block vote are significantly silent when it happens to be cast in accordance with their own views.

Criticism is directed against the method of choosing the Executive. There are those who constantly demand a more vigorous and active leadership. There is a current but, I think, erroneous idea that the rank and file are always ahead of the leaders. I do not agree. One has to remember that there is only a small proportion of people who are continually interested and active in politics. They are reinforced in industrial disputes by many who are normally content with nominal membership. They are on the political side strengthened by many who are interested in the fight just as they are interested in other forms of sport. These may also from time to time be swayed by enthusiasm, but have normally other interests that absorb them. The keen member is apt to mix mainly with those of like mind. He may easily gather quite a wrong impression as to the strength of feeling. The propagandist going from meeting to meeting is apt to judge the feelings of the people by the response which he gets, not remembering how relatively few are those who come to meetings. It is the task of those who are called upon to lead to try to stimulate enthusiasm and to direct it in the desired course, but they must keep in close touch with the rank and file so that they may know how far they can be carried with them.

Those who are always wondering why the Executive does not run campaigns on this, that, and the other do not realise that there is a limit to the amount of work of this kind that can be carried on, and that if it is overdone the law of diminishing returns applies. A more serious complaint is that the Executive is too large and unwieldy for the rapid despatch of business. It is suggested that, meeting only once a month, events move too rapidly for it. There is some truth in this complaint, but, as a matter of fact, when quick action is necessary, the Finance and General Purposes Committee, or, in a sudden emergency, the Chairman and Vice-Chairman, often act, and look to the Executive for subsequent endorsement. Here much depends on those who occupy these positions. The practice for many years has been to appoint a chairman for one year only, and to select him or her by rotation, the choice falling upon the member who happens to have had the longest period of service. There is undoubtedly grave disadvantage in this system. Mere length of service on an executive does not necessarily imply that a person is a good chairman of conference or even of an executive. Chairmanship has a technique of its own. It has happened on occasions that the Chairman of the Party who has had to face serious difficulties either at the Conference or in the everyday work of the movement has been a person of no particular ability or standing. There is much to be said for getting a chairman of greater permanence for administrative work, and allowing the senior member of the Executive in rotation to be made president for the year with perhaps the right of delivering an address at the Annual Conference.

There is much criticism directed against what is called " Transport House." Much of it is not deserved, but it must be admitted that all political head offices are apt to develop certain tendencies. I find that the kind of criticism directed by the Labour Party against officialism is not unknown in the Conservative Party in relation to their central organisation. There is necessarily developed in such organisations a certain amount of routine, officialism, and caution. All officials like to have a quiet life and are apt to be impatient of those who do not fit in smoothly as cogs in their machine. They all tend to be conservative in regard to their methods and to regard innovations with suspicion. This is not unnatural when one remembers the amount of ill digested suggestions which they receive from members. Much of the criticism of headquarters is unfair because critics assume that there is money available to carry out their schemes. Transport House has to cut its coat according to its cloth, which is generally very scanty.

PARLIAMENTARY CANDIDATURES

The influence of the Trade Unions is, perhaps, greatest in the sphere of the choice of parliamentary candidates. In the early days of the movement, except for a few members supported by the I.L.P., the bulk of the Parliamentary Party were nominees of the Trade Unions, who paid for the constituency organisation, the election expenses, and also, before payment of members, were responsible for parliamentary salaries.

Every candidate endorsed by the National Executive must have responsible financial backing. This comes either from the Trade Union or from some other affiliated body, or from the funds of the local Labour Party. The finance of the big Unions has enabled them in the past to secure for the Trade Union nominees many of the safest seats in the country, and in the selection of candidates up till recently they had a considerable pull, owing to the fact that they were able to take responsibility for all expenses.

A recent decision of the Party Conference, has, however, restricted the amount of money which may be paid by organisations or by individual candidates so that this undesirable competition has now been limited.

The selection of parliamentary candidates is a matter entirely for the constituency organisation. Provided that the candidate selected has the necessary qualifications, the National Executive cannot interfere with the decision, nor can they in any way force a particular candidate on to a constituency Party. They have, however, the right to suggest names, and this is frequently done.

Often constituency Parties approach the head office for advice as to the choice of a candidate.

Formerly, agents tended to be the servants of particular organisations, rather than of the Party as a whole, but considerable progress has been made in reforming this practice.

Much criticism is directed against the Labour Party on account of its choice of candidates. It is suggested that there is a tendency to put into Parliament men whose experience has lain mainly in the industrial field, and that not enough chance is given to others. There is some truth in this criticism. It is difficult to steer a clear course between getting too much freedom in the local organisations and giving too much authority to the National Executive. In my view it is essential that the constituency Parties should have the greatest possible freedom of choice, as there would always be a tendency, where the Executive had control, to lean to safety rather than brilliance, and orthodoxy rather than ability.

THE PARLIAMENTARY LABOUR PARTY

The Labour Party in Parliament is governed on democratic principles. It consists of all Labour members who are prepared to subscribe to the standing orders which have been laid down by the Parliamentary Party itself and can be revised by it. These bind members to conform to the decisions of the majority, although, where there is a question involving conscientious conviction, the members are given the right to abstain from voting. There have been attempts to suggest that there is something wrong in this insistence on a Party pledge. It is thought to turn a representative into a mere delegate. In fact it is only a recognition of the duty of a member to represent his constituents. A Labour candidate stands for certain definite principles, and is supported by men and women who have chosen him to represent them and to carry out these principles. They have, therefore, the right to expect that he will faithfully carry them out. As a matter of fact the pledge is only an honest and explicit avowal of the discipline which is necessary for all effective work in Parliament by a political Party. The Conservative member who votes against his Party may be dealt with even more drastically than the Labour member unless his personal position makes him too formidable to be tackled by the Party authorities. The real difference is that the Labour member takes part in the decision by which he is bound.

At the beginning of every session a leader, deputy-leader, and whips are elected by vote of the members. In addition about a dozen members are elected to form, with the three chief officers of the Party, an executive. This executive, which is responsible to the Parliamentary Party, meets almost every day during the session while the whole Party meets at least once a week. Party action in the House is therefore decided by the whole body of the members. Between Party meetings the executive decides, or, if it cannot be assembled, the leader or member in charge of business on the floor of the House takes decisions. In practice a considerable degree of latitude is given to members, and the Party shows much toleration of individual vagaries. It insists, however, on majority rule. It was on this point that the members of the I.L.P. seceded. They claimed, in effect, that they were better judges of what was Party policy than the members.

Action in the House is a matter for the Parliamentary Party, the members of which decide on the application of Party policy. The Labour Party Executive is the body to interpret policy between Conferences, but in its own sphere the Parliamentary Party is supreme. To members of the Labour Party this machinery may seem natural, but in Parliament it was an innovation. In the old Liberal and Conservative Parties far more power is conceded to the leader. He appoints the whips and decides who shall be members of " the Shadow Cabinet." Full Party meetings seem to be held by the Conservative Party only in times of crisis, and then at the will of the leader. Lord Balfour's *Life* shows how successfully during the days of the split over

Tariff Reform he was able for months to avoid calling one.

The Labour peers also have regular meetings, are represented on the Parliamentary Executive, and have the right to attend Party meetings. The National Executive has the right to attend Party meetings at the beginning of every session and take part in discussion.

The Parliamentary Labour Party necessarily has some of the defects as well as the advantages of democracy. Obviously where there is a concentration of power in the hands of one man or of a small group it is possible to act with greater rapidity and secrecy than in a Party where all important matters are submitted to the judgment of the rank and file. On the other hand the average member of the Party is better informed on the pros and cons of the questions which arise and is a more responsible member than many of those in other Parties, who are content to accept policy from their leaders and orders from their whips.

The machinery of the Labour Party provides for the ventilation of grievances and for the alteration of policy or tactics in accordance with the will of the members. Criticisms can be made openly and replies made to them. Every year also there is the opportunity of changing leaders and of altering the composition of the Executive. There is, therefore, no need for the cataclysmic changes which are necessary under autocratic rule. The method of annual elections also allows of the Front Bench being reinforced by those whom the Party thinks worthy, instead of promotion being in the sole hands of a leader.

The Leader of the Party in the House is also the Leader of the Party in the country, and is *ex officio* a member of the National Executive. This body generally contains a number of M.P.s, so that there is a close liaison between the two authorities. Now and again, when it is desired to arrive at a joint decision, meetings are held of the three executives of the National Party, the Parliamentary Party, and the Trade Union Conference. When Labour was in office the Party elected a consultative committee from the rank and file to keep in touch with the Ministers.

I have set out at some length and in detail the constitution of the Labour Party because even among some of its adherents there is a good deal of ignorance as to the actual machinery whereby the Party functions. Although there are heard from time to time allegations that the Party is bossed by a strange entity called " Transport House," the real complaint might be made that the elaboration of machinery makes the Party slow in action and that this is due to the care with which all vital decisions are made by the rank and file through their representatives.

Critics often forget how extremely difficult it is to devise a constitution which will do this and at the same time work rapidly and efficiently. Democracy is the hardest form of Government. In the long run it depends on the constant activity of the individual. The vitality of the Labour movement depends on the members of the local Labour Parties and the Trade Union branches. If they fail in energetic action the movement may tend to become mechanical. The driving force of a democratic movement must be derived from the sum of the enthusiasm of the members. If this is wanting no efforts from above can replace it.

CHAPTER V

LABOUR PARTY METHOD

The Labour Party has deliberately adopted the method of constitutional action and has rejected the tactics of revolution. I have endeavoured to show in Chapter I the historical reasons for this. I have traced the growth of the Labour Party from small beginnings to a position in which it challenges the Capitalist parties. Under pressure of that challenge the minor differences between Liberals and Conservatives have practically disappeared. The formation of the National Government marked the end of an epoch. Henceforward the issue that confronts the electors of this country is Socialism versus Capitalism. The Labour Party believes that, when it has obtained the support of a majority of the electors for its policy, it will secure the acquiescence of the greater number of its opponents in the changes which will be brought about.

There are, however, those who claim that Socialism will never be introduced without a violent struggle. They believe that, as soon as it is found that democracy is no longer prepared to be the handmaid of Capitalism, the supporters of the present system will reject it. They think that any attempt to deal with fundamentals will be met by forcible resistance. They think that parliamentary action is only useful as a preparation for an inevitable struggle that will be fought out, not at the ballot-box, but with bayonet and bomb. It is idle to deny that there is this possibility. The last few years have seen the overthrow of democracy in many countries and the development of Fascism, which is only a cloak for Capitalism. It is, however, unwise to argue from the experience of one country to that of another. There is nothing more misleading than to try to apply to all countries a cast-iron theory of historical necessity and to argue that Britain must go the Moscow road unless she follows the example of Berlin or Rome. The theorist at the end of the eighteenth century might equally well have argued that Britain must go the way of France unless she was prepared to align herself with Austria and Prussia. I do not suggest that there is not a possibility of an attempt by reactionaries to seize power by force. I am well aware how slight a hold the principles of democracy have on some of our opponents, but I believe that the vast majority of the people of this country reject such methods, and that an attempt of this kind would be defeated by the loyalty of the mass of the people to the Government.

I believe that a violent struggle in this country would be extremely dangerous to civilisation, whichever side ultimately conquered. British Socialists have always recognised the conflict between classes but have not generally adopted the class war as a theory of society. It is, of course, true that there is a vital conflict in the community between the classes that live by mere ownership and those that live by labour, but it is not nearly so clear-cut and distinct as is sometimes imagined. There are not just two sharply contrasted classes, Capitalists and wage-earners. Between the man who owns nothing but his labour and the man who depends entirely on unearned income there are many grades of people, some of whom are predominantly workers while others are predominantly Capitalists. In this country there are many workers who own some property; there are many Capitalists who do useful service to the community. The method of violent revolution implies the subjugation, if not the extermination, of those classes which are opposed to Socialism. It implies in reality the acceptance of the totalitarian State. I do not accept the totalitarian State as desirable as an end, and I believe that an attempt to achieve it by force brings with it very great evils.

The attempt by one section of the community to dominate all others inevitably means the adoption of terrorism as a weapon. This can be seen in Fascist Italy and Nazi Germany, but it is also evident in Communist Russia. Once the method of terrorism is adopted it is very difficult to abandon it. In theory, the period of terrorism and dictatorship is transitory. In practice, it continues. In Soviet Russia to-day, fifteen years after the cessation of foreign intervention, the method of terrorism continues, as may be seen from the trials of the Trotskyists. However much the leaders of Soviet Russia desire to escape from it, they cannot, because the methods that gained power continue to be employed by those who now seek to attain it. In the totalitarian State a forcible rebellion is the only way to effect change.

In this country there have always been small sections who advocated a forcible revolution, but they have found but little favour with the majority of the people, because such methods are alien to the national temperament. For years there were those who hankered after the romance of the barricades and the rising of the people against their oppressors. The changes in the methods of destruction due to the progress of science have made these dreams further and further from reality.

The Labour Party does not seek to establish a drilled and dragooned community where only one opinion is allowed. On the contrary, it realises that the wealth of a community is its diversity, not its uniformity.

I believe that the people of this country are as unlikely to accept Communism as Fascism. Both systems appeal to the politically immature. Both are distasteful to peoples like the British and French, who have had years of experience of personal freedom and political democracy.

While, as I have stated, the Labour Party has steadily opposed the tactics of revolutionary action and violence, and has always pinned its faith to constitutional action, it has never ignored the possibility that occasions may arise when extra-parliamentary action may become necessary. Its faith in constitutional action inevitably depends on its opponents also adhering to it. As long as the workers have it in their power to achieve their ends by the use of the ballot-box, they have no right to seek to obtain them by other means. If Labour cannot obtain a majority, it must as a minority accept the will of the majority. It may seek to influence that majority, and those to whom it has entrusted power by every lawful means, but to try to enforce its will on a majority by violence is contrary to its democratic faith. Stated thus, the proposition seems simple, but in fact there are borderline cases which require more examination.

It may be that the Government which has received a mandate from the electors deliberately goes against or beyond the wishes of those from whom it has derived its power. It may be that it behaves so tyrannically that it drives a minority to revolt. The question then arises as to whether a position may not occur in which it is right for a minority to bring pressure to bear on a Government by direct action of some kind or other.

Thus a Government might, in defiance of its election pledges, take action which amounted to aggression leading to a war. It might deliberately disregard public opinion in the matter. It might ignore its manifestations and continue on a course which was bound to involve the whole nation in great loss and suffering, if not ruin. It may be, then, right and necessary for a minority to take action, but it must be recognised that at that stage the method of constitutional action has been abandoned. A revolutionary situation may result.

THE GENERAL STRIKE

The particular form in which this question has been discussed by the Labour movement has been that of the general strike. For years it has appeared on the agenda of national and international conferences, and its justification, efficacy, and limitations have been discussed. It has been advocated from the undemocratic point of view as a method whereby the class-conscious workers might seize power by force. In this form it has had little support in this country. It has been advocated as a method whereby a disfranchised class may obtain the vote or redress electoral inequalities. In the case of Belgium it has actually been exercised successfully. More frequently it has been advocated as the last weapon in the hands of the workers to prevent them being dragged into a war against their will, or as a means of countering a *coup d'état*. For these purposes it has had its successes. In 1905 the Norwegians sought to free themselves from their union with the Swedes. There was a possibility that the more powerful country might seek to preserve the union by force. The threat of a general strike by the Swedish workers was a powerful factor in bringing about a peaceful settlement. In 1920, in Germany, the attempted *Kapp Putsch* was defeated by a general strike of the workers. In this instance the general strike was used in support of the constitutional Government. In 1920 in Britain the Coalition Government was engaged in an endeavour to overturn the Soviet Government. The Hands Off Russia campaign, which forced the Government to withdraw from their adventure, derived much of its force from the knowledge that the very powerful and active Trade Union movement might take direct action.

Here, indeed, one sees the real effectiveness of the general strike. It is most powerful when not used. The knowledge that a particular course of action may lead to its use has often been very effective in influencing the action of Governments, especially in negativing attacks on labour. It is in its actual use for positive achievements that difficulties arise. There have been those who have thought that by constant threats of strike action great advances might be won, but in fact sooner or later those who threaten find themselves compelled to act. Either they give way, which blunts the weapon even if it does not make it useless, or they are compelled to act. Once action is taken the issue is widened. The sphere of revolutionary action approaches. The thing becomes a trial of strength between two forces. Victory depends ultimately on the force of public opinion, or even on sheer physical endurance.

The idea of the general strike in this country derived much of its strength from a widespread belief that a Government would not resort to extreme violence. It was action conceived in terms of conditions which have largely passed away. The power of a Government which possesses arms is infinitely stronger to-day than ever before in history. The weakness of unarmed and undisciplined masses is relatively far greater. At the same time the callousness and ruthlessness of the governing classes is immeasurably greater than in the half-century which preceded the Great War.

The general strike has often appealed to the pacifist as a way in which force can be used without violence, but the result seldom fulfils his expectations. Theoretically a Government might be brought to its knees by the passive resistance of the masses, but in practice the use of the strike weapon on a national scale inevitably merges into violent strife. The reason is obvious. The strike weapon in action always hurts those who use it. Inevitably the poor are hit by the privations which it brings. Unless a general strike is successful very rapidly, there is a growing discomfort, and even suffering, which exacerbates feelings on both sides.

It is perhaps only in this country that purely industrial strikes can be carried on for weeks and months without violence, and this is only achieved with great difficulty.

THE POPULAR FRONT

It is generally admitted that the position of a Government which cannot command a majority in the House of Commons is one of great difficulty, although it is often forgotten that for many years in the middle of the last century this condition obtained. During the period in which political parties were leaving the old alignment of Whig and Tory for the new one of Liberal and Conservative there was seldom a stable majority.

Nevertheless, Governments of the day managed to function and to carry out their legislative programmes. This was due to the fact that there was no real line of demarcation between parties. It is true that on either flank there were groups of Left Wing and Right Wing extremists who differed profoundly, but even these did not differ in their fundamental conceptions of society, while amongst the great mass of members and electors differences were rather those of individual conviction on particular points than on broad lines of political or economic theory. It was at that time possible for a man of the distinction of Gladstone to be invited to join a Tory or a Whig Government without the circumstance causing any surprise.

We have in our own time seen Coalition Governments formed both in time of war and peace. The war-time Coalitions stand in perhaps rather a special category. In time of war there is one overmastering issue which may effect a union of people who differ widely in their conceptions of society but are united in the resolve to defend the particular society to which they belong. It may even happen that the threat of danger from outside may enable a Government comprising very heterogeneous elements to unite on a policy of national safety, as may be seen at the present time in France, where the *Front Populaire* includes not only Liberals and Socialists but also

Communists, and Radicals who are from the British standpoint Conservatives. In France, it is true, the people are quite unaccustomed to any one party having a majority, and have been governed for years by the temporary coalition of separate groups. In this country, however, a minority party can only govern by suppressing its individuality and compromising with other parties. The short-lived Labour Governments of 1924 and 1929 were dependent on the neutrality, if not the active support, of parties which differed from them on fundamentals. They were, therefore, in the position of being unable to implement the policy in which they believed, and could only survive by not challenging the fundamental standpoint of their opponents and seeking to secure such changes as could be achieved within the framework of the existing order of society. This is also the professed basis of the *Front Populaire* in France.

The Labour Party stands for such great changes in the economic and social structure that it cannot function successfully unless it obtains a majority which is prepared to put its principles into practice. Those principles are so far-reaching that they affect every department of the public services and every phase of policy. The plain fact is that a Socialist Party cannot hope to make a success of administering the Capitalist system because it does not believe in it. This is the fundamental objection to all the proposals that are put forward for the formation of a Popular Front in this country.

There are many people who suggest that what is required at the present time is the formation of an alliance between all the Left Wing forces in order to get rid of the present Government. The argument is based sometimes on the need for getting through certain urgent reforms in home affairs, sometimes, and perhaps more frequently, on the plea that at all events all can unite on a common policy in foreign affairs, and that on this basis it would be possible to rally a majority in this country for what is vaguely called a Left Government. Many people stress the purely negative attitude—that is to say, the urgent need of getting rid of the present administration before, through their feeble and dishonest policy, they allow the world to be plunged into war. Others believe that it is possible to form a short-term policy to which the various Left Wing groups would give their adhesion, and that upon this basis electoral arrangements could be made which would ensure a majority.

I would not myself rule out such a thing as an impossibility in the event of the imminence of a world crisis. It might on a particular occasion be the lesser of two evils, but it is worth while examining these proposals in some detail, because they have an appeal to many who do not in my view look far enough ahead.

I will first deal with the purely negative proposal which considers that the really vital thing is the extrusion from power of the present Government. I should be the last person to underrate the importance of this, but the overthrow of the present Government means its replacement by another. You cannot simply leave a vacuum.

A majority of heterogeneous composition returned on a negative policy of turning the Government out, with a clear foreign policy but no programme for home affairs, would not last more than a few weeks. Even where foreign affairs overshadow the political scene, the day to day work of a Government is mainly concerned with administration and legislation on internal affairs. The essential support that a Government needs is not for a few major issues, but for the ordinary common round and daily task. The first essential for a Government which has to work through the House of Commons is command over time. More things are lost by delay than by open opposition. The elaborate machinery of the Whips Office, and the discipline imposed on the supporters of a Government, are essential if it is to function at all. This discipline, although enforced by pains and penalties, by hopes of reward and by the fear of dissolution, depends in the last resort far more on a realisation by the members of the relative importance of particular issues. The discipline imposed by membership of a party not only in the House of Commons, but in constituency party work, is a reflection of a general appraisement of the value of the attainment of certain aims, and a willingness to subordinate the particular points on which the individual feels keenly to the general sense of the Party. It is, in fact, the acceptance of the fundamental principle of democracy—majority rule.

It has never been easy to obtain this discipline in parties of the Left. Parties of the Right tend to contain fewer individualities, while their members in this country have been drilled by the nature of their upbringing to the acceptance of what they would term the team spirit. Parties of the Left tend to be composed of enthusiasts for particular reforms who hope by joining with others to achieve their aims, and of men and women who have through their individuality come to the front, rather than those who by the possession of wealth or position have drifted into politics. Thus the Liberal Party always tended to be fissiparous. It always included in its ranks a number of what are called impolitely " cranks "— that is to say, enthusiasts for various good causes. The party was kept together by the large body of persons who were traditional Liberals, or perhaps even without any marked convictions except an interest in politics and a desire to make a career.

In the Labour Party, the Trade Union element serves as the solid core of disciplined membership. The loyalty to majority decisions, which is the foundation of industrial action, takes the place of what is called among Conservatives the team spirit, while long training in the responsibilities of Trade Union work has induced a habit of mind which realises the practical necessity for compromise in non-essentials. A further link which makes for united action is the common faith in Socialism which inspires the members. There are, however, always a few who, while convinced Socialists, have as their main incentive devotion to some particular reform. Their enthusiasm for their own special cause is apt at times to make them lose their sense of proportion. There are also, naturally, some members whose fervent desire for the achievement of their ideals makes them impatient of the delays and partial successes which are inevitable in working through the methods of parliamentary democracy.

The experience of the two Labour Governments showed how difficult it was for many of these to accept the compromises inseparable from all Government, but particularly from a Government in a minority. There was needed to give the experiment the degree of success which it attained the full force of party loyalty and of devotion to the cause of Socialism.

But if there is to be an election resulting in the

return of a majority consisting of several minorities united only on a negative, the Government will be intolerably weak. If the groups are in themselves strong and coherent, it may be possible, by the inclusion of leaders drawn from all of them, to obtain a fairly consistent support, but at best the battle will only be transferred from the floor of the House and party meetings to the Cabinet Room. The larger the party the greater its sense of responsibility; the smaller the group the more irresponsible. The largest party becomes at once the prisoner of the minority groups, which put all the pressure they can to ensure decisions in the sense which they desire.

Within the coalition there is a rivalry. There is a temptation always for the smaller groups to show themselves more advanced than the main body. This tendency has been very fully illustrated by the action of the I.L.P., which, rejoicing in irresponsibility, is always able to outbid the Labour Party, because it is not bound to realities. If to the I.L.P. and the Labour Party were added a group of Liberals fundamentally at odds with Socialists on aim and a group of Communists fundamentally opposed on method, the prospects of long life for the Government would be small.

Many of these objections apply equally to the suggestion that there should be a positive programme to which all organisations on the Left should adhere. It is thought that many Liberals might accept a limited programme of certain specific items calculated to be carried through within the life of one Parliament, and that upon this basis a Left Government might be achieved at an early date. It is thought that there is a large body of Left opinion which, while unwilling to commit itself to Socialism, is yet prepared to accept a considerable instalment of the Socialist programme. It is commonly suggested that enough work for one Parliament could be found without going beyond the limits which would repel adherents of the Capitalist system.

It must be admitted that there is considerable strength of opinion in support of this proposition, and I think that there is ground for the view that there are many in this country who are prepared to go a long way with the Labour Party while not prepared to take the plunge and join any affiliated organisation. It is, therefore, worth while examining this proposition.

The first question that arises is as to the limits of the programme which would be acceptable. I find that the proposition often reduces itself to this—that if the Labour Party would drop its Socialism and adopt a Liberal platform, many Liberals would be pleased to support it. I have heard it said more than once that if Labour would only drop its policy of nationalisation everyone would be pleased, and it would soon obtain a majority.

I am convinced that it would be fatal for the Labour Party to form a Popular Front on any such terms. It may be possible in other countries, but not in this. I have stated above that Socialists cannot make Capitalism work. The 1929 experiment demonstrated this. No really effective steps could be taken to deal with the economic crisis, because any attempt to deal with fundamentals brought opposition from the Liberals. Labour men who saw clearly the need for dealing with causes had to try to deal with results. The amount that could be extracted for the workers from a Capitalist system was limited. When this limit had been reached, failure was bound to ensue. I admit that the experiment was not made under fair conditions. The Party was handicapped by the conditions of the time, which demanded drastic measures, and by its leading personnel, who had surrendered their minds to Capitalism long before they sold their bodies.

Therefore any such short programme to be acceptable to Socialists must contain measures which will take the country a long way on the road to the desired goal. It must contain a big instalment of nationalisation. The subjects of nationalisation must be not those about which there is little controversy, because they are not vital, but those which are really vital for the transformation of society and are called for in the national interest. I shall indicate later what I believe these to be, but I do not know how far it would be possible for any large number of Liberals to accept them.

Next, there must be a development of the control of the community over trade and industry, which runs counter to the shibboleths of individualism. I do not underrate the value of the suspicion of bureaucracy which the Liberals exhibit. It is, indeed, necessary that Socialists should import into the structure of the society which they are building what is valid in Liberalism, but I have the impression that Liberal elements in a Popular Front Government would baulk at necessary controls.

With this there must be a steady pressure exerted through the medium of the Budget, wage standards, social services, etc., towards a more equalitarian society. I return to the point which I made above—that in the carrying on of a Government it is all-round support that is required. A Socialist Government must inform its whole administration with the Socialist ideal. All its Ministers must be conscious of the goal to which they are steering the ship of State. It is just here that I see the crux of the situation. In a Popular Front the Socialist elements are definitely out to replace Capitalism by Socialism. They work with that aim in view all the time. If, on the other hand, they have colleagues or supporters whose conscious aim is the preservation of

Capitalism, there cannot possibly be harmony.

There are those who will say that this is a playing with words; that "We are all Socialists now"; that there is no absolute Socialism or Capitalism; that it is all a matter of degree and so forth. I cannot accept this. Socialism to me is not just a piece of machinery or an economic system, but a living faith translated into action. I desire the classless society, and the substitution of the motive of service for that of competition. I must, therefore, differ in my outlook from the man who still clings to the present system. Even though we agree that, say, the mines should be nationalised, we disagree with the end in view and with the reason for our action. He regards the mining industry as an exception to the general way he wishes to carry on industry. He thinks that owing to the history and conditions of the industry it had better be nationalised, but he still regards it as a profit-making undertaking. I, on the other hand, conceive it as a basic activity of the community for providing certain necessary needs, and as but the first of many services which must undergo a transformation.

THE UNITED FRONT

The difference of end makes it hard to work with the Liberals; the distinction of method makes it practically impossible to work with the Communists.

LABOUR PARTY METHOD

The demand for a United Front, which is being pressed with considerable vigour at the present time, has naturally a very strong emotional appeal. The spectacle of the workers who ought to be united against their opponents fighting among themselves is naturally disheartening to those who see the dangers of the times in which we live, and who are full of enthusiasm for the cause of Socialism. They are apt to think that the difficulties in the way of forming a United Front between all sections of Socialists are due to the vested interests of the reactionary tendencies of those who hold office in the Labour Party and the Trade Unions. They imagine that a great victory is possible if only unity can be achieved.

I share their distaste for internecine warfare between Socialists and their desire for unity, but that unity must be real. It is no use patching up a sham unity between people who differ fundamentally. I do not share their belief that lack of unity is due to personal ambitions or to individual shortcomings on either side. I think these differences of opinion are sincerely held by supporters of the Labour Party and dissentients alike.

What is the fundamental difference which keeps these men and women, sincerely desirous of achieving Socialism, from uniting? It is this. The Labour Party believes that the Socialist movement must be democratic, and that the will of the majority must prevail. The dissidents do not. The members of the Independent Labour Party broke away from the Labour Party on this issue. They claimed that, while belonging to the Party, they must be free to decide when the Party was or was not acting in conformity with Party policy. They claimed the right of individual action when they thought that they were right and the rest of the Party wrong. All Labour Party decisions are made by majority vote. The Leader of the Parliamentary Party is not entitled to act contrary to the decisions of the Party, any more than the National Executive is entitled to ignore the decisions of Annual Conferences. The I.L.P., in effect, claimed to be possessed of some innate superiority which enabled them to decide more rightly than others. This claim could not be admitted. The I.L.P. can rejoin the Party at any time when it chooses to accept the obligations which are binding on all other members.

The case of the Communist Party is somewhat different. Its members sincerely believe in a method of action which is rejected by the Labour Party. They think that the method of constitutional action is mistaken. It is, of course, an arguable proposition, but it is quite incompatible with whole-hearted support of the Labour Party. The Communist Party, further, is not a free agent. It is subject to the orders of the Comintern. It, therefore, does not admit that the Annual Conference of the Labour Party must be the deciding authority, and that those who have been elected to carry out its decisions must have the necessary authority. Its willingness to enter the Labour Party is, therefore, subject to these two qualifications. It does not believe in the methods of the Labour Party and it does not really accept majority rule. Its whole philosophy is based on the seizure of power by an active minority. Like the I.L.P., it is undemocratic. It believes in rule by those who are superior to ordinary people—in fact, by an ideological aristocracy. I regret the loss to the Labour Party of the services which its members might render, but their very devotion to their particular tenets necessarily makes it impossible for them to work whole-heartedly in the Labour Party.

The case of the recently dissolved Socialist League was again different. Its members appeared to accept the policy of the Labour Party except on the question of the formation of a United Front. This policy had been rejected by Conference. It was, of course, open to any member of the Party to continue to work for its acceptance, but it was not open to him to do exactly what Conference had decided should not be done. The error of the members of the Socialist League was, again, a rejection of majority rule. They claimed to know better.

These three bodies are not large, compared with the Labour Party. They profess a great desire for unity, but in fact the unity which they desire is to be on their own terms. If, as a matter of fact, working-class unity is of such vital importance, it can be secured quite easily by the few thousand dissidents agreeing to fall in with the majority of millions. What is claimed, however, is that the great majority should submit to the views of a small minority.

I am not prepared to arrogate to myself a superiority to the rest of the movement. I am prepared to submit to their will, even if I disagree. I shall do all I can to get my views accepted, but, unless acquiescence in the views of the majority conflicts with my conscience, I shall fall into line, for I have great faith in the wisdom of the rank and file.

CHAPTER VI

SOCIALIST OBJECTIVE

THE AIM OF THE LABOUR PARTY is the establishment of the Co-operative Commonwealth. Its object, expressed in the Party constitution, is " to secure for the workers by hand or by brain the full fruits of their industry and the most equitable distribution thereof that may be possible, upon the basis of common ownership of the means of production, distribution, and exchange, and the best obtainable system of popular administration and control of each industry or service."

In this chapter I want to explain what is my conception of the kind of society that is there envisaged. I am not going to try to picture a Utopia or to give a detailed sketch of what society will be like under Socialism. However useful such an exercise of the imagination may be, it is out of place in this volume, which has only a limited aim. Further, any picture of a Socialist society is subject to this disability—that it gives a static appearance to something which is of its very nature continually in process of development.

There is not some particular state of society on arriving at which one can say, " Finality has been reached." Some future historian will not be able to point to a particular date as that on which the Socialist State was established, in the same way as the United States of America dates from the Declaration of Independence, because Socialists envisage human progress as continuous. The goal which we are striving to reach to-day will only be the starting-point for our successors. Socialism is not an end itself, but only the means of attaining conditions under which the fullest possible life will be available for the human race. Further developments which we cannot contemplate to-day will inevitably follow.

The most that can be done to-day is to show the principles that will be applied in endeavouring to build up a new state of society, to mark clearly the next steps which must be taken, and to indicate the necessary features which will be displayed in the next stage.

I am not in this chapter dealing with the methods of attaining to the Socialist State, nor with the immediate programme which the Labour Party proposes to fulfil as the first step to that end, but rather with the general aims of the Socialist movement, and the kind of society that its adherents wish to see.

FREEDOM

The first point which I desire to make is that the aim of Socialism is to give greater freedom to the individual. British Socialists have never made an idol of the State, demanding that individuals should be sacrificed to it. They have never accepted the beehive or the ants' nest as an ideal. They leave that to the advocates of the Corporate State. They have never desired that men and women should be drilled and regimented physically and mentally so that they should be all of one pattern. On the contrary, they appreciate that the wealth of a society is in its variety, not its uniformity. Progress is not towards, but away from the herd. It is no part of the Socialist idea that there should be in every human activity an orthodox pattern to which all must conform.

This is well illustrated by considering the attitude of the Labour Party towards religion. In the Labour Party are found active adherents of many religious creeds, and also men and women who do not conform to any denomination. There has never been any attempt to impose on members of the Party a creed of materialism, any more than there has been any imposition of a religious test. Within the Labour Party everyone is entitled to hold what religious views he will. Where legislation impinges upon religious questions the individual member is accorded complete freedom of action. It is recognised that religion is a sphere which should be left to the individual.

Again, in education, while Socialists have protested against a bias in favour of the existing order being maintained in education, they have not sought to twist education into a means of imposing upon all a rigid orthodoxy. They have such faith in the rightness of their views that they desire the utmost freedom of enquiry and discussion. The action of the Nazi Government in Germany in turning their universities into parrot cages for the repetition of the catchwords of Fascism evokes only contempt. The tendency observable among Communists to try to reduce all history to an economic formula has always been rejected. The conception of a proletarian art and literature which must be sharply distinguished from anything hitherto accomplished in those fields is quite alien to true Socialism. It results from a sense of inferiority. British Socialists recognise very clearly the danger that exists in the tyranny of the reformer who wishes to make all men in his own image. The very differences which arise in the Labour movement are an earnest that in the Socialist State of the future there will be constant vigilance to prevent loss of freedom.

State action is advocated by Socialists not for

its own sake, but because it is necessary to prevent the oppression of an individual by others, and to secure that the liberty of the one does not restrict that of others, or conflict with the common good of society.

Those who attack Socialism on the ground that it will mean the enslavement of the individual belong invariably to the class of people whose possession of property has given them liberty at the expense of the enslavement of others. The possession of property in a Capitalist society has given liberty to a fortunate minority who hardly realise how much its absence means enslavement. The majority of the people of this country are under orders and discipline for the whole of their working day. Freedom is left behind when they " clock in " and only resumed when they go out. Such liberty as they have got as workers has been the fruit of long and bitter struggles by the Trade Unions. But a far greater restriction on liberty than this is imposed on the vast majority of the people of this country by poverty. There is the narrowing of choice in everything. The poor man cannot chose his domicile. He must be prepared at the shortest notice to abandon all his social activities, to leave the niche which he has made for himself in the structure of society, and to remove himself elsewhere, if economic circumstances demand it. This is called " transference." How little would those who so easily recommend this to the workers appreciate being transferred from their pleasant homes in Surrey or Buckinghamshire to Whitechapel or the Black Country. Yet this is an ordinary incident of working-class life. The poor man is restricted in his food, his clothing, his amusements, and his occupation. The liberty which it is feared Socialism may restrict is the liberty of the few. Moreover, in modern Capitalist society, the power of wealth is such as to affect the lives of the people in thousands of ways. The whole organisation of the country is based on the superior rights of the wealthy. Nothing is sacred to the profit-maker. The beauty and amenities of the country are at his mercy. The life of whole communities may be ruined at his will.

Yet one other vital deprivation of the poor must be mentioned. Leisure, which is the essential thing for the living of a civilised life, is only tardily being recognised as the right of those who work for the community, and is even now miserably insufficient for the majority. Even a fortnight's holiday with pay is exceptional. The result is that for the majority the social heritage of the race is locked up. The two keys, time and money, are not within their reach.

The liberty which Socialists desire is liberty for all. The restrictions which will be imposed will be those only which are essential to secure it. The current misconception of a Socialist society as one in which everyone will be subject to the constant interference of an army of officials is due to the fact that in order to avoid the worst abuses of Capitalism society has had to institute a whole series of services of inspection to check the anti-social actions of those engaged in private enterprise. Factory inspectors are necessary because many employers lack social sense, just as " speed cops " are needed because many motorists lack road sense and a feeling of responsibility to the community. Their presence is not due to the Socialist but the anti-Socialist spirit.

It is true that in the Socialist State people will be deprived of the right of living in idleness at the expense of the community, but this right is in practice denied to the majority already by their economic circumstances. On the other hand, when the community is organised for service instead of profit there will be no such thing as the enforced deprivation of the right to work which is now imposed on nearly two million people in this country at the height of a trade boom, and on many more whenever there is a slump. The denial of the right to work is one of the greatest infringements of liberty imposed under Capitalism, for it deprives the individual of the right of expressing his personality and exercising his functions as a citizen.

My conclusion is that men and women will be more free, not less free, under Socialism. Freedom will be more widely disseminated. There will be no attempt made to impose rigid uniformity. There will be no forcible suppression of adverse opinion. The real change will be that a man will become a citizen, with the rights of a free man during his hours of labour just as in his leisure time. This does not mean that he will have the right to do just as he will. He will have freedom within the necessary restraints which life in a complex society imposes.

SECURITY

One of the most serious charges that can be made against Capitalism is that it fails to give any sense of security to the vast majority of people. There are a few who have, through the possession of property, achieved complete security from the threat of poverty. But they are very few. The overwhelming number of people in every Capitalist country live in constant fear of losing their only means of livelihood through causes entirely outside their own control. Depending as they do entirely upon the sale of their labour, they may at any time find themselves without buyers, owing to a temporary breakdown in some part of the Capitalist machine. Some people have, of course, accumulated savings during the time that they have been at work, but a comparatively short period of unemployment will use up the average working man's savings, and leave him and his family without any means of subsistence except such relief as may be afforded by the State.

The establishment of Socialism will bring about a fundamental alteration in this condition of affairs. A Socialist State cannot afford to allow men to remain idle. As soon, therefore, as there ceases to be a demand for a man's labour in one direction, he will be given some other kind of work to do. He will be certain that as long as he is capable of making a contribution to the national wealth he can be sure of a job, and of sufficient money to keep himself and his family at a reasonable standard of living.

EQUALITY

Socialists do not propose to substitute the domination of society by one privileged class for that of another. They seek to abolish class distinctions altogether. The abolition of classes is fundamental to the Socialist conception of society. Whatever may be the professions of belief in democracy made by supporters of the present system, they do, in fact, think it right and natural that there should be class distinctions. This is the attitude not merely of those at the top, who appear to benefit by the present order, but of the Conservative working man also. As part of the joy of the blessed in the old conception of heaven was the contemplation of the miseries and torture of the damned, so there are people who seem to be unable to derive satisfaction from their own worth unless they can contrast it with the inferior position of others.

Society to-day is so ordered that there is a struggle between classes, between those who derive their living from the ownership of property and those who are dependent on their labour. This class division is not, however, as clear-cut as some theorists assume. There is much subdivison into grades. Those who are in the higher grades of society would resent being lumped together with small tradesmen and professional men as common members of a single Capitalist class. Similarly, the solidarity of the workers is limited by quite a considerable amount of class distinction, although many old divisions based on pride of craft or of occupation are now disappearing.

Although, on the whole, class distinctions are less than they were, owing to the breaking down of the barriers of birth, there remains the great factor which divides people into social classes—that is, inequality of wealth. It is not so much the actual possession of wealth which makes for division as access to a certain standard of life which the ownership of money affords.

Socialists do not propose to level down, but to level up. There is no particular virtue in equality in misery and squalor. It is mainly false sentimentality which talks of noble poverty. It is now possible for all to enjoy a reasonably high standard of life. One of the striking features of present-day society is the existence of very low standards of life which are not imposed by the inability of the community to provide better. They are not even necessitated by the demands of the well-to-do for luxuries. They are caused simply by the failure to utilise resources which are available. Without reducing the standards of life of the wealthy, a great advance in the material well-being of the masses is possible, but this is not enough. The existence of wide disparities of wealth, with a consequent segregation of the community into separate classes, is inimical to a true social life. To abolish classes altogether is not so chimerical an undertaking as it would have appeared some years ago. During the past few decades there has been a levelling up of education, culture, and social habits. The gulf which formerly separated the manual worker and the brain worker has narrowed. The dividing-line between classes is far more one of economic circumstances than of cultural differences. Under Socialism the aim will be to utilise the services of all citizens in the way which will be most conducive to the benefit of society and to the individual, and to give to all who render service approximately equal advantages. Equality does not, however, mean identity. Human beings are, of course, unequal, and have diversities of tastes and gifts, but this need not be expressed in wide social inequalities.

No doubt it will be some time before substantial economic equality is achieved, but ultimately it must be. There is no way of measuring the value of the services rendered by those who work in various ways for the community so as to give a greater reward to one rather than to the other. No doubt habit and custom will survive for some time. It is, I think, unlikely that complete uniformity of hours of work will be attained. Some will work longer than others, but have compensating advantages. All will not necessarily have the same amount of purchasing power. The aim, however, of the Socialist State must be equality. This must be the guiding principle applied in its plans of organisation.

DEMOCRACY

I have already stressed the belief of the Labour Party in democracy. In these days, when modern industry and commerce demand the co-operation of a great army of individuals who are entirely unknown to each other, and when, owing to the close integration of world economy, the fortunes of every individual are dependent upon the actions of other people in his own country and abroad to a greater extent than ever before, there is a tendency to regard the problems of politics and economics as too difficult of comprehension for the ordinary man. The average citizen finds himself to be but a cog in a great and complicated machine. He cannot control or even understand it. He is inclined to leave the task to others. Hence has arisen the despairing demand for dictatorship. There seem to be many who have the herd mind. They desire to choose some old bull to follow. Unfortunately, the old bull is generally both stupid and bellicose. There is every indication that he will lead the herd to destruction.

Socialists reject the conception of dictatorship altogether because it is powerless to effect that which they wish. They are not concerned solely with material things. They do not think of human beings as a herd to be fed and watered and kept in security. They think of them as individuals co-operating together to make a fine collective life. For this reason Socialism is a more exacting creed than that of its competitors. It does not demand submission and acquiescence, but active and constant participation in common activities. It demands that every individual shall shoulder his or her responsibilities.

It would no doubt be easier to plan a new organisation of society in which all controlling power would be entrusted to a few super-men by whose orders, through an obedient bureaucracy, the material resources of this country, or even of the world, would be developed, and the activities of all the peoples directed to produce certain results. Provided that there were sufficient faith in the wisdom of those directing affairs, such a society might make rapid material progress, and might endure for a time, but it would be subject to all the dangers and uncertainties which accompany dictatorships, not the least of which is the mental instability which seems almost inevitably to attack dictators. I do not believe that there are human beings who are fit to be entrusted with such absolute power. I believe, too, that such a society would be spiritually very poor. The really fatal objection to any such plan is the absence of all power of changing the régime. Democracy involves the right to change the policy and personnel of those to whom government is confided. Without this right there is no true freedom. Its denial throws all dissenters from the existing order back to violence as the only remedy. The apparent stability of a dictatorship conceals this real weakness. Where the only possibility of change is by violence, the Government is bound to protect itself by intense police activity. It is inevitable that all dictatorships, whether of the Left or the Right, should be police-ridden States, with the invariable accompaniments of espionage, delation, and terrorism. The insistence on the maintenance of democracy by the Labour Party against those who advocate dictatorships, whether on the Berlin or the Moscow model, is founded upon a deep conviction that any divergence from it involves loss of liberty. Liberty once surrendered is very hard to recapture.

I hold, therefore, that despite the inevitable disadvantages in slowness of action which observance of democratic methods involves, it is necessary to make provision at all stages in the organisation of the Socialist State for the active participation of the citizens and for the exercise of control by them directly over their immediate activities, and indirectly through their representatives over the wider policy of the State. Such control involves the freedom to make mistakes. The idea that the ideal State is one in which no mistakes are made seems to me wrong. Unless there is the liberty to err there is no freedom. Democracy necessarily involves some loss of immediate efficiency, but in the long run makes for its increase. I conceive that in the Socialist State there will be, besides the democratic framework of the State and of industry, a great variety of voluntary societies controlled by the members, wherein all the time a training in democracy will be taking place. There will always be a certain number of people who are unwilling to take responsibility, or whose minds are absorbed in other things, but the success of the Socialist State will depend on the active participation of the greatest possible number in the making of decisions.

It is sometimes suggested that the manager and the technician will be unable to function because of the constant interference of committees of workers or consumers or others. I do not believe this. The genius of the people of this country does not lie in the elaboration of theoretical constitutions but in their practical ability to make them work. The introduction of democracy into industry will give another field for the exercise of this genius. Experience has, I think, shown that, despite the divergence of aim incidental to the Capitalist system, it has been possible in many industries to get wide co-operation between workers and management. I have no doubt that this will be so when the principal bone of contention is removed.

COMMON OWNERSHIP

Land will be owned by the community, not by private individuals, but the citizen will have reasonable security of tenure; in fact, he will be far more secure than are the majority of people at the present day, who are liable to be turned out of their dwellings at the will of a landlord or forced to abandon the homes that they have made through a change in their economic circumstances.

All the major industries will be owned and controlled by the community, but there may well exist for a long time many smaller enterprises which are left to be carried on individually. It is not possible to lay down a hard and fast line on the constitution and management of every industry. There will no doubt be wide diversity in accordance with the requirements of particular undertakings. One may, however, lay down certain essential conditions. The first of these is that the interest of the community as a whole must come before that of any sectional group. The second is that the managers and technicians must be given reasonable freedom if they are to work efficiently, a freedom within the general economic plan; while the third is that the workers must be citizens in industry and not wage slaves. The exact way in which this will be worked out will again depend on the circumstances of particular industries. In the organisation of industry there are to be considered the interests of the community as a whole, the interests of the producers, and the interests of the consumers. Each interest has its particular sphere in which it must be paramount. The organisation of the Labour movement is triple—the Labour Party, the Trade Union movement, and the Co-operative movement. There is, therefore, already in the

Labour movement a recognition of these three separate interests, and constant practice in reconciling them. The problems of socialised industry will, therefore, be faced by those who already understand the difficulties and the dangers to be avoided.

There is one great danger that must be avoided —over-centralisation. Great Britain is suffering at the present time from the too great concentration of population and of economic and financial power in London. A Socialist Government will plan for the whole country, but within the general plan there must be local application.

Just as with individuals, so with the country, there is a danger in uniformity. Capitalism is to-day actively engaged in making the whole country uniform. Chain stores, cinemas, and banks, and masses of houses of uniform type, take the place of the distinctive features which gave charm to the countryside. Cheap newspapers and cinemas have the effect of filling people's minds with the same narrow range of ideas. I conceive that under Socialism there will be a wide regional decentralisation, and a deliberate endeavour to allow for each area to express the individuality of the people. In particular there must, of course, be decentralisation in Scotland and Wales. One of the vital problems of the present day is to reconcile the natural claims of nationality with the larger interest of the world as a whole. It may be claimed that in Great Britain the world has been given an example of how three races without losing their national characteristics can combine in a larger unity.

If this success is to continue it must be by giving due weight to the claims of the separate nationalities to preserve their own culture and develop their own national life. True Socialism does not mean an internationalism that ignores the diversities of different peoples, but in recognising them and providing for their expression.

INVENTION AND PROGRESS

At the present time inventions almost always bring unmerited sufferings on persons whose livelihood depended on the continuance of things as they had been. Scientific invention, instead of giving increased satisfaction, often means increased insecurity. This does not mean that scientific invention and technical progress are wrong, but that under private enterprise they are used, not for the general good, but for the advantage of a few. Invention and progress are often hindered by vested interests, which prevent the development of new ideas because they threaten the profits of existing undertakings. Under Socialism there will be no need to suppress inventions, because every device for increasing wealth or easing labour will result in the raising of the general standard of life and comfort. A Socialist Government will, therefore, foster research, and give full scope to the application of new inventions. No group of persons will have a vested interest in particular economic processes, and no persons and no districts will be allowed to suffer through a change in industrial activity.

BEAUTY

One of the heaviest indictments against the Capitalist system is that it is destructive of beauty. The widespread ugliness in Britain is the result of putting profits first. Socialists regard economic activities only as the foundation for a full life of the spirit. It is not surprising that so many artists and poets are found in the Socialist ranks. They realise that, until the pressure of material needs is relieved, it is difficult to get people to think of life in terms of beauty. As long as there are wide divergencies of wealth and class divisions in society, false ideals will prevail. One of the greatest tasks for those who are striving to build up a new society is to extend the horizon of the ordinary man and woman. Under present conditions it is often deplorably narrow. It is to be feared that many of those who support the Labour movement do not see much beyond one step upwards in the social scale. Nevertheless, it is something to see thus far, for there are many people in this country who are still pathetically content with the standard to which they have become accustomed. Every step forward means a wider vision. People who do not yet see much beyond, so to speak, the amenities of a London suburb will from that point progress further. There have always been in the ranks of the Socialist movement plenty of people who are discontented with narrow and immediate achievements. I am glad that it should be so, for without continual striving for something better retrogression is certain.

A Socialist Government, while seeking to increase wealth, and while utilising science and invention to lighten the task of the human race, will not be content with a material success. In planning the new Britain they will think of it, not just as a basis for wealth production, but as the environment in which men and women are to live happily and finely.

NATIONALISM

"National Socialism" is a contradiction in terms. A true Socialist cannot allow his sympathies to be bounded by anything so narrow as a nation, for nationalism is only egotism writ large. It follows that it is impossible for a Socialist Government to pursue a foreign policy that is at variance with its principles. It would be so doing if it attempted to create ideal conditions for the people of its own country at the expense of others. I have already stressed the point that British Socialists do not adhere to an ideological imperialism which would impel them to try to force all other nations into a common mould. Just as, in forming the new social order at home, the ruling principle is not to enforce uniformity but to give individual freedom, so in dealing with external affairs a Socialist Government will recognise the right of each nation to regulate its own affairs according to what it considers desirable, provided that in so doing it does not conflict with the general interests of the human race. In dealing with the other constituents of the British Commonwealth, full effect will be given to this principle. The process whereby the Dominions have become equal partners with the mother country, so that their continued association has become entirely voluntary, must be continued until the commonwealth consists only of free self-governing units. The old idea of class distinctions between the various peoples which are united under the British Crown, distinctions based on colour, race, or history, must give way to equal partnership. Economic exploitation of one territory by another must no longer continue. Equally, in the larger sphere of foreign affairs a Socialist Government will work for the utmost freedom for every nation within the larger unity. Just as a satisfactory social system can only be achieved by the surrender of the absolute right of individuals to do as they please to the interests of the whole community, so, in the world, peace and prosperity can only be secured by the surrender of absolute sovereignty of nations to the common interest of civilisation. It is not by insistence on the absolute rights of nations to do what they will that peace will be secured, but by co-operating in the provision of common services and by the development of common standards. The Socialist looks to the World Co-operative Commonwealth, not as some distant ideal, but as something which must be realised if mankind is not to perish by his own inventions.

I have in this chapter given a brief outline of the kind of Britain and kind of world which I want to see. I have done so, not because I think that I can see very far ahead, or because I think that I can paint in words an attractive picture. This has been done by many others with far more qualifications. I have done it because I want to emphasise two things. The first is that I believe that it is necessary for everyone to think out as clearly as possible what kind of a world he wants and then to consider what is the best way to attain to it. The second is that the Labour Party has its immediate programme, which it intends to carry out whenever it is given power to do so. This programme is directed towards the attainment of some such state of society as I have sketched. It is intended definitely to begin to make those fundamental changes necessary for its realisation. It is based on the principles which I have indicated. I believe that a Socialist Government must have always very clearly before it its ultimate aims and ideals. It must work throughout with the object of attaining them. It must not rest content with minor successes. It must, even when dealing with immediate problems, keep in mind always the goal to which it is tending. It is here that the Labour Party is so different from those parties which believe fundamentally in the retention of a class system of society and in a Capitalist system as the economic foundation of society. They see a form of society in existence which they think to be right although it may require some alterations. Socialists see a society which is wrong and which must be replaced by another. From this it follows that the approach of a Socialist Government to the problems which it has to meet is altogether different from that of its opponents. The latter, accepting things as they are, can be content with patching the old garment. The former must have a definite plan, and must from the start work to make that plan a reality.

THE ENGLAND WE WANT TO SEE

The new order of society will enable millions, who up to now have had to toil in factory and workshop all their lives without any prospect of ever experiencing the good things of life, to get their first opportunity of enjoying some of those luxuries that are now confined exclusively to the well-to-do. Let us consider for a moment the sort of life that we hope will be led by a working man and his family under Socialism.

A great part of the week, under Socialism as under any other system, will inevitably be spent in work. Whether that work is in factory or office, the worker will be able to feel that he is working in his own concern, which belongs to him as a British citizen. He will know that the work he is doing will be of benefit to himself and to every other person in the country. There will be no question of the goods he is producing being destined for destruction as " surplus " because the economic system cannot absorb them. Everything that is made will add to the sum of the country's wealth. He will know, too, that if he continues to work satisfactorily there is no chance of his losing his job. In fact, he will feel that his employment is secure, and that he is contributing to the prosperity of his country. The knowledge that the factory belongs to him will not be confined to a vague and indefinite feeling of ownership. He will, through his union, be able to have a say in its management. If he finds that the conveyor belt is being run too fast, or that the precautions against accidents are not being properly observed, for example, he will be able to take action at once with a view to getting the matter remedied. In a thousand and one ways he will feel the difference between working for a private Capitalist and working for the nation.

Important as will be the change in conditions inside his office or factory, this will only be a part of the profound alteration that Socialism will bring about in his life. It will, as I have said already, give him a far greater degree of leisure than he has known in the past. But leisure is of little use unless it is accompanied by sufficient means to utilise it to the full. The unemployed to-day have "leisure" enough and to spare, but they are deprived of the means of enjoying it. The worker under Socialism, with a forty-hour week and holidays with pay, will be able to use his leisure to the full. New avenues will be opened up to him that to-day are closed through the failure of the Capitalist system to provide a living wage for all.

There are few workers to-day, for example, who can afford to travel. The vast majority have to remain within a short distance of their homes, and never have an opportunity of seeing the world. A reorganised national transport system, providing cheap fares by road or rail for those who want to spend their holidays in visiting other parts of their own country, would revolutionise the average worker's holiday time.

To-day, however, if a working-class family does go into the country for a day, it is, as a rule, simply to travel along road or rail through other people's territory. One of the great changes that will come about in a Socialist Britain will be that large areas of land will be set aside as national parks, in which people will be free to enjoy themselves without being prosecuted for trespassing on private property. In these parks there will be rest-houses, where it will be possible for people to come and stay during their holiday, and camps where they can send their children to get all the benefits of fresh air and sunshine which are denied to the great majority of children living to-day in crowded streets.

Not everyone wants to travel, however, and there are many who may still prefer to stay at home. But they want "home" to be a place that they can be proud of. To-day there are many homes that are simply four walls, and have none of the amenities that they could have if full use were made of all those inventions that science has placed at our disposal. The aim of Socialism will be to see that every family in the country has a house with electric light, and power for cooking, central heating, refrigerator, and plenty of floor-space, one in fact that is well furnished with everything that a modern housewife needs. All this may sound utopian, but if we realise that there are men in the building and allied trades out of work, and being paid by the State for doing nothing, it begins to sound more reasonable.

Finally, there are those who want to develop their own minds further, and secure for themselves the education that they need in order to have a full appreciation of all that is meant in the much misused phrase " culture." To acquire this knowledge costs money. To-day only a limited number of people can afford to educate themselves or their children. A few of the latter, who show exceptional brilliance, may get scholarships, but the vast majority have to be content with what they have learnt at elementary schools. A great extension of educational opportunity both for children and adults would make a profound difference in the lives of numbers of our countrymen. Such an extension is one of the aims of Socialism.

These are just illustrations of the kind of opportunities that Socialism will bring to the average working-class family. There are a hundred others, ranging from a good square meal to a trip to the Continent. All of them may be summed up in a sentence, by saying that we mean to give every man, woman, and child in the country an opportunity to live the fullest life that the resources of our island will allow.

CHAPTER VII

SHORT PROGRAMME

IN THIS CHAPTER I want to consider a practical programme for a Labour Government coming into power in this country. It has its general objective—the establishment of the Socialist Commonwealth. It must take the first steps for its realisation, but at the same time it has to deal with immediate and pressing evils which call for remedy. It has to work, not under conditions where everything has to be rebuilt from foundations, nor in an atmosphere of complete calm where it can work entirely on a long-term programme of reconstruction. It will come in backed by the demands of its supporters for immediate relief from the economic evils from which they suffer. It cannot concentrate on major measures of Socialisation alone, the result of which will not be apparent for some time; it must satisfy the immediate needs of those who suffer from unemployment, low wages, long hours, bad housing, malnutrition, and many other evil things which are the concomitants of Capitalism. Any programme of action must therefore be made up of short-term and remedial items and long-term and constructive measures. In attempting to set out what a Labour Government would do, one has to realise that one is working without full knowledge of the conditions.

In the first place, one does not know what may be the state of affairs at home or abroad. It may be that Labour will come to power at a time of acute tension in international relations which will necessarily absorb a great amount of its attention and energy.

Secondly, it may be that Labour will come into power at a time when the trade cycle is in decline, when there is rising unemployment and acute distress. In that event immediate ambulance work may be so urgent as to prevent far-reaching measures being put in hand immediately. On the other hand, the seriousness of the economic condition may make it possible for a Labour Government to increase the *tempo* of change because the people will appreciate that drastic remedies are necessary. Such was the position when President Roosevelt came into power in the United States. He was able to initiate experiments which in normal times would have been intensely repugnant to the majority of Americans. The depth of the economic distress gave him the opportunity and the support for drastic action.

Thirdly, it is impossible to tell with what

majority Labour will be returned. The speed and extent of its activities will necessarily be conditioned by the amount of support which it has behind it. We have already had the lesson of the difficulty of a Labour Government in a minority doing really effective work. A Government with a very small majority would also be seriously handicapped.

I must therefore make some assumptions in considering what a Labour Government would do. I will assume that economic conditions when Labour attains to power are normal—that is to say, that the country is enjoying fairly good trade, which means, under Capitalism, that the unemployed are round about two million, and that the majority of the people are unable to obtain, with their purchasing power, enough food to keep them in full health, or enough house room for comfort, or a really adequate supply of the material bases of existence. I will assume that world conditions are fairly quiet—that is to say that the world consists of a number of armed nations suspicious of each other and spending a great deal of their wealth and labour on warlike preparations, but that at the moment there is no immediate danger of an outbreak.

I will assume that the Labour Party has been returned with a working majority and a clear mandate from the people to put into force its programme. What should it do ?

THE MACHINERY OF GOVERNMENT

It is worth while considering first the nature of the machinery with which a Socialist Government will have to do its work. The system of government and administration in this country has been evolved through the centuries and adapted from time to time to new conditions. There have been at times doubts as to whether it could function with success during periods of great changes. Despite many difficulties it has worked. It has, indeed, worked far better than many systems which have been framed with strict regard to logic and theoretical perfection. Without violent change, power has passed from one class to another, from the landed interest to the capitalists. Government, once the monopoly of a few, has been extended to the many. It is my belief that with this machinery we can bring about the fundamental changes which we desire, provided that we continue in this country to respect the will of the majority and to practise the principles of democracy.

The Labour Party, as I have said before, is firmly based on democracy. It is utterly opposed to dictatorship. It detests a system of government in which only one view is allowed to be heard and in which the administration is not subjected to the healthy criticism of an Opposition. It is, therefore, resolved to preserve the essential fabric of the

British system of government. This does not mean, however, that there is not need for improvements in procedure. The machinery of our Parliament was devised to meet wholly different conditions from those which obtain to-day. The House of Commons was for many years engaged mainly in checking the Executive, which was not fully responsible to it. It was not devised for the efficient and speedy despatch of public business. Its procedure was developed during the nineteenth century, when the conception still held sway that the less the Government did the better. Much of this procedure is undoubtedly time-wasting and ineffective. At the same time it is not easy to alter the form without losing the spirit, because it has been built up, not on theory, but on practice. It has achieved a very difficult thing—that of giving the Government of the day the power to get through its business, while preserving to the Opposition a full opportunity of discussing legislation and criticising administration. It can, as a matter of fact, given a certain amount of reasonableness, work with considerable despatch. On the other hand, if an Opposition chooses to obstruct deliberately, it can cause great delay or even wreck the machine.

A Labour Government will not allow its programme to be wrecked by factious obstruction, but it will not trample on the rights of a minority.

There are, I believe, certain changes in

procedure which would give the members of the House greater opportunities of service, would not restrict the rights of an Opposition, would make for greater efficiency, and would enable a bigger output of legislation to be secured. Some of these changes are too technical to be described here. The most essential change is the proper allocation of time, especially on committees, by the use of an agreed time-table. Where both sides agree to this, experience has shown that time is saved and only important matters discussed. A fuller use of committees would also save time which is now often wasted by discussing details in Committee of the Whole House.

I do not think that a Labour Government should waste much time over elaborate attempts to alter procedure, but should only make such alterations as are really necessary for effective work.

THE HOUSE OF LORDS

The probable opposition of the House of Lords to the Labour programme must be faced resolutely. The Labour movement has no desire to obscure the economic issues which it presents to the country by staging a constitutional struggle, but it will make it abundantly clear, whenever it goes to the country, that in seeking a mandate for its policy, it seeks also authority to make that policy effective. It intends to secure that the will of the people, as expressed at the polls, should prevail. It will not allow its measures to be whittled away by amendments in the House of Lords, or to be subjected to delay. Should the authority of the people be challenged, it will demand the ending of an anachronistic survival. The procedure of the Parliament Act is not effective. Time is the essence of the carrying out of a programme. A Labour Government cannot afford to wait in impotence while its measures are held up.

All the arguments in favour of a second chamber rest upon the assumption that there is something fundamental which must be preserved against the will of the electors. In some federal constitutions the Upper House is designed to secure the rights of the federal units. In this country the House of Lords has no such function. In effect it exists to preserve, no matter what Government may be in power, the continuance of a system of society based on Capitalism and class privilege. The feebleness of the action of the Liberal Party when challenged by the Lords is explained by the fact that Mr. Asquith no less than Mr. Balfour was in favour of the existing basis of society; but the argument has no validity for a Socialist Government. Whatever may be the case for continuing some piece of machinery for reviewing and making technical suggestions for the amendment of legislation before it is finally passed, there is no case from the democratic point of view for having any constitutional obstacle to the decision of the people prevailing.

THE EXECUTIVE

There is another piece of machinery which is in urgent need of reform if effective work is to be done without needless delay. The Cabinet now usually consists of twenty-two people, most of whom have heavy departmental charges. They meet every week to dispose of a crowded agenda wherein figure items of very different importance and urgency. Its members are to a great extent concerned mainly with particular items.

The Cabinet, as now constituted, sins against the first principle of good administration, in that it does not distinguish between the function of planning broad strategy and making decisions as to the detailed execution of plans.

The system worked fairly well when the content of Government was small. It may function where the main lines of policy are merely the acceptance of what is, but it will break down if it is to be made the instrument for the execution of a plan of reconstruction. It is, in my view, essential to make a distinction of function between Ministers who are responsible for detailed administration and those to whom is entrusted the work of dealing with the broader issues. There are a number of Ministerial posts which have no very heavy departmental duties, but as a rule these are assigned to persons whose inclusion is desired either on account of their representative capacity or as an acknowledgment of past services and distrust of their administrative abilities. Frequently these persons are mere passengers in the boat.

These posts should be filled by Ministers who have the faculty of directing broad issues of policy. They should be in charge of functions not departments. Each should, in his own sphere, be, so to speak, the representative of the Prime Minister in relation to a particular group of services, and should preside over a committee of the Ministers charged with administration. Thus the general co-ordination of the social services would fall to one Minister. Defence would be the care of another, economic policy of a third, and external relations of a fourth. There should be a continuous contact between these Ministers. The Prime Minister is necessarily the responsible head of the Ministry, but he needs to be assisted by a small group of members of the Cabinet whose specific function is co-ordinating policy and giving general direction. This does not mean the supersession of the Cabinet by a small *Junta* and the relegation of departmental Ministers to an inferior status. On the contrary, the Ministers who are charged with co-ordination will be in constant and close contact with the Ministers in their respective groups, who will, through them, be able to make their views felt more effectively.

In particular I believe that the junior Ministers should be able in this way to make their influence felt. At the present time there is a serious defect in our governmental machinery in the absence of a general staff as contrasted with the staff of the particular Ministries. The Prime Minister has no department. He has only private secretaries and the very small Cabinet secretariat. In order to carry through a co-ordinated plan of reconstruction, there will be required a well-equipped and diversified staff at the centre to work out the main lines of the plan which is to be implemented in the departments. The creation of the Economic Advisory Council was a recognition of the need for a central organ, but its basis was wrong. It gave an opportunity to a Prime Minister who had no clear policy to find excuses for inaction. A Government should not require advice from experts as to what policy to pursue. What it needs is expert assistance to carry out its decisions. A Labour Government, having achieved power, will have no doubts as to the policy to be pursued. It will have its plan of reconstruction which it will proceed to achieve.

THE PLAN

The Labour Government will not dissipate its strength when returned to power by dealing only with minor matters. It will proceed at once with major measures while its mandate is fresh. It will initiate measures in every department of Government designed to fit in with a general plan. This general plan is based on the principle that it is the business of the Government to see that the resources of the country, material and human, are utilised so as to produce the greatest amount of well-being for all. I use the word "well-being," not "wealth," because wealth is apt to be considered as relating only to material things, whereas under the term "well-being" I include all those things that go to make up a good life. Thus in striving to develop to the utmost the production of wealth, it is necessary to consider the conditions of wealth production and their effect on the producers. If increased wealth production involves such an expenditure of energy as impairs the ability to enjoy it, it is wasteful. To sacrifice leisure to luxury is false economy.

I say "for all" because here is the essential difference between Socialist planning and Capitalist planning. There are many advocates of a planned economy who join with Socialists in denouncing the waste and chaos of wealth production. They would seek to substitute for the anarchy of competitive industrialism a planned and organised system, but they still retain their belief in a class society. Socialists believe in a classless society, and the plan which they put forward will envisage a steady progress towards greater equalisation of wealth. In considering what it is desirable to produce in this country they will consider who are to be the consumers. It is no use planning production for a society with its present gross inequalities if your intention is to develop society more and more on lines of equality.

A plan based on the principles indicated above involves four main lines of direction. First, the planning of industry in order that there may be produced those things which are required in the right quantities. Second, the location of industry —that is to say, a decision as to what economic activities shall be carried on in the various areas of the country so as to make the greatest use of natural advantages and the social capital invested in those areas with due regard to the interests of the people who inhabit them. With this goes a decision as to the amount and character of the agricultural production which it is possible and desirable for this country to maintain. Thirdly, a decision as to the best utilisation of the workers of this country, so that those who are by their age and qualities most fitted for work should be employed, while the old and the young should be resting from or training for their labours, and fourthly, a decision as to the standard of life which this country can afford to its citizens, and the amount of production of capital goods which is required and the direction of capital into those channels where it will be most advantageous. It is, therefore, necessary that the Government should have at its command the best available information in order that it may plan wisely.

When these decisions have been made it is clear that the Government must have the necessary powers to implement them. Some of these powers are already in the hands of the Government, and only the will and the vision are lacking. The distribution of purchasing power is continually being affected by Government action. Every year in the Budget, decisions are made involving the taking of purchasing power from one set of people and giving it to another. A rise in the income-tax, coupled with an increase in the old age pensions, is a move towards equalisation. A tax on tea, and the lowering of the rate of supertax, is the reverse. But continually, by quotas, subsidies, and tariffs, money is being taken out of one pocket and put into another.

This form of governmental action of which we have seen so much in the last few years is also of effect in making decisions as to the amount and character of production. Numerous tariffs and subsidies have been imposed in order to induce production of this or that commodity. Most of these devices have been determined by the pressure of private interests. It is possible that some of them might be utilised by a Labour Government for purposes of national planning, but these methods are seriously defective in that they seek to do by a control of private interests what can be done effectively only through State action.

Similarly, there are on the Statute Book Acts which properly used can affect the distribution of work and leisure among various sections of the population. These, too, can be put in operation. But despite these encroachments by the Government on the sphere of private enterprise, the main controls of the economic system remain in the hands of those whose actuating motive is private profit. It is to the securing of these controls for the service of the community that the Labour Government will turn its hand.

FINANCE

First in importance is financial power. Over and over again we have seen that there is in this country another power than that which has its seat at Westminster. The City of London, a convenient term for a collection of financial interests, is able to assert itself against the Government of the country. Those who control money can pursue a policy at home and abroad contrary to that which has been decided by the people. The first step in the transfer of this power is the conversion of the Bank of England into a State institution.

No proposal of the Labour Party has been subjected to such gross misrepresentation as this. It is the measure of its importance. It has been suggested that the object of the proposal was to seize the savings of the well-to-do. Such is not the object, nor, indeed, could such an object be effected by it. It is control of the money power which is aimed at. Presumably now that France and New Zealand have nationalised their central banks we shall have less of this kind of talk. It may, however, be as well to emphasise that the Bank of England will continue, as at present, to be operated by a skilled staff, for the impression has been given that it will be operated by members of Parliament or Ministers. The day-to-day work of the Bank will be carried on by officials, but the general policy and direction will be controlled by the Minister. Through the Bank of England it will be possible to control the joint-stock banks and ensure that credit policy will be in line with the policy of the Government. When taking over control of the Bank of England provision will also be made for securing that credit shall be available and capital be directed into the channels of most advantage to the community by the creation of a National Investment

Board. This will enable the Government to finance large schemes of national development such as Housing, Electrification, Transport, etc., and the establishment of new industries.

THE LAND

The Labour Party stands for national ownership of the land. As long as private ownership exists it is impossible to prevent the values created by the community from being absorbed by the landlords. It is equally impossible to plan the development of the country in the national interest so long as there is obstruction by the landed interest and so long as every piece of social development has to pay a heavy toll to monopolists. The Labour Government will, therefore, pass a measure giving power to purchase compulsorily whatever land it requires for whatever purpose. There are a number of powers to purchase land for particular purposes already in existence, but no general power, while its acquisition involves long delays and expensive procedure. It is vitally necessary that a Government that means to carry out a great programme should not be delayed at every step. The measure will provide for the taking over of land within the shortest possible time consistent with due regard for the position of the occupier and user. The exact terms of compensation can be decided on after possession has been gained provided that the owner is not deprived of the income which he draws from it.

COMPENSATION

It is at this point that it is necessary to lay down clearly Labour's point of view on compensation. The Labour Party believes in paying compensation during the period of transition towards the Socialist Commonwealth as part of its conception of the method of change. Confiscation is part of the technique of revolution not of constitutional action. There are two reasons why it is wise to compensate: the first is ethical, the second practical. During the process of reconstructing the basis of society which must necessarily take some years, it is not equitable to penalise the persons who happen to own the property which comes early in the list of those things which the State determines to acquire. There are those who attach a moral obliquity to the holding of certain kinds of property such as land, mining royalties, or brewery shares, and they desire to punish such property owners. It is not, however, possible to draw these distinctions between various owners. The owner of land may have recently acquired it by giving in exchange the savings of a lifetime of hard work. The owner of some form of property which it is not proposed to take over immediately may have made all his money from owning slum property, but have recently sold the one and acquired the other. Confiscation is a form of taxation differing only from any other tax in the amount taken. The Socialist canon of taxation is to tax according to amount, not according to the source from which that wealth comes, except in so far as it is necessary to distinguish between earned and unearned income. Confiscation is apt to hit the small man as well as the big one whose iniquity bulks large in the eyes of the reformer.

The second reason is one of expediency. It is stupid to arouse unnecessary antagonism. In this country, while the division of wealth is grossly unequal, there are, nevertheless, a mass of workers who own some property. Their interests are with the workers, but if they are deprived unjustly of their reasonable expectations they will feel the injustice acutely. A few cases of gross injustice to individuals will outweigh in the public mind the greater injustice done to the workers collectively. Further, it is of the essence of constitutional change that reasonable expectations should be respected and that the transition to the new order should be as smooth as possible. The violent denunciations of the method of compensation come only from irresponsibles.

Therefore, in all cases where the State finds it necessary to take over private property, reasonable and just compensation will be paid. The redressing of inequalities of wealth must be effected through taxation. The process cannot be combined with nationalisation either equitably or expediently.

COAL AND POWER

The third direction in which control must be exercised is in respect of fuel. Of all the industries which might be taken over and converted into a national service, that which is concerned with the nation's fuel is most urgently in need of reconstruction, in the interest both of the nation and the workers employed therein. Coal has been the foundation of our industrial development. It is one of our greatest national assets. We depend on it largely for our power, light, and heat. Yet we allow this great business to be shamefully mismanaged, and we are content as a nation to sweat the men on whose dangerous and heavy toil we depend. Quite apart from any other considerations, the condition of the depressed areas is largely due to the state of the coal industry, and no real remedy can be applied until this essential factor is set right.

The position of the coal trade provides a good illustration of the principles on which the Labour Government will proceed. Looked at in terms of national economy, the coal industry performs two services to the community. First, it provides the source from which light, heat, and power are drawn, whether by the use of raw coal or through the production of gas, electric current, or oil, and is also a valuable raw material for the chemical industry. Secondly, it is an article of export in exchange for which we buy much of our food and raw material. We can, if we will, produce for ourselves by the labour of our citizens enough heat, light, and power for industrial and domestic use. The price which we charge for this service to the consumers depends on the degree of skill with which we organise the production and distribution, and the remuneration which we give to the producers. To some parts of the fuel-producing industry we have applied control. Prices are to some extent limited in the gas and electricity industries. A large proportion of those industries is owned and controlled by the community. The workers are not exposed to competition, and their products, except in so far as they are in competition with imported oil, have a monopoly.

Raw coal, however, is competitive in the home market and internationally, and the wages of the workers are depressed owing to world competition.

The Labour Party will take over the whole coal industry and reorganise it on the basis of giving adequate wages and good conditions to the miner. The price of coal, whether to the ultimate consumer or to the industries which utilise it for further production, will be based on this first claim of the worker in industry. The organisation of the industry will be placed in the hands of a board, and it will be correlated with the gas and electrical supply industries, both of which are ripe for complete nationalisation. The internal price of coal need not be affected by the world price. It is a matter for decision as to how much coal we should sell abroad. Coal is only one of the commodities which we give in exchange for our imports. The Coal Board will get the best prices that it can, whether in competition or, preferably, by international agreement, but, whichever it is, there is no reason why it should affect the wage of the miner. In a nationalised economy the price of coal, except in so far as it may affect the competitive power of industrial consumers, is a matter of internal arrangement.

It is clear that, if the fuel industry is to be organised on a sound basis, there must be control of imported fuel, especially oil. By fixing the prices of the various kinds of heat, light, and power in accordance with what is most suitable in the national interest, a great degree of stability can be introduced into our national life. It will be a matter for decision, into which factors of relative economy, national planning, and defence will enter, as to how far we should endeavour to produce in this country all the oil which we require.

In the organisation of the fuel service the workers will play their part, as has been explained in the policy adopted by the Party. With stability introduced into the coal industry, the problem of the distressed areas can be dealt with. The extent of the industry can be decided and the exploitation of fuel resources planned in an orderly way.

TRANSPORT

The fourth great service which is ripe for transformation into a national concern is transport. At the present time it is the sport of contending interests. Sometimes it is the motor industry, with the powerful oil interests behind it, which gains a point; sometimes it is the railway interests, so strongly entrenched in the Conservative Party. Meanwhile the chaos continues.

The Labour Government will proceed to nationalise the railways and other main forms of transport, including aerial transport. There will, no doubt, remain for a long time much transportation in private hands. The Labour Government is not proposing to take over the individual's car or the business man's fleet of lorries, but to organise the main transportation services of the nation. Here, again, the basis must be the proper remuneration and conditions of the workers. For years the nation exploited the railwaymen just as much as we sweat the miners to-day. At the present time the grossly excessive hours worked by drivers of motor vehicles sets up an undesirable competition with the railways, prevents a proper organisation of transport, and adds to the dangers of the road.

Proper planning of transportation needs foresight. It needs to be related to the planning of industries and also of amenities. A national system of transport can be used to assist in the proper location of industry and also of the control of the growth of towns. In a small country such as England it is vital that we should not waste what we have. Equally important is the making available to all of the amenities in which this country is so rich. The Labour Government will be thinking and planning not only for work, but for recreation. There is urgent need for the provision of national parks in order that the leisure which is now attainable, provided that we utilise the advantages which science has placed in our hands, should be used to advantage.

Road, rail, and sea transport should not be regarded as separate undertakings. They form part of a single whole. At the present time there is nothing to prevent one port being neglected and another developed according to the immediate interests of profit-makers. There is a scramble for business between the various agencies so that goods which ought to go by rail go by road, and vice versa. In a short time the development of air services will bring yet another competitor into the field. The Labour Government will end this chaos. Here again the same principle will be adopted as in taking over other industries. The function of management will be performed by those best fitted to do it, but their activities will be pursued within the general framework of the policy laid down by the Government. This policy looks, not to one form of transport, but to transport as a unified service. It looks, not to transportation by itself, but to transportation as one of a number of functions essential to the life of the community. Instead of being an end itself, it is but part of the machinery which keeps going the life of the people. It serves the interests of industry and agriculture, and must be adapted so as to fit into the general scheme. The essential change that will take place will be the change of motive from profit to service and the change from sectional interest to the interests of the community as a whole.

These, then, are the first four great tasks which the Labour Government will undertake. It is worth while considering and dealing with some objections.

OBJECTIONS

There is, first, the idea that somehow or other the Government will make a loss if it tries to run these undertakings. This is, of course, due to an entire misunderstanding of the situation. The community to-day runs the roads at a heavy expense. We think it worth while to give up part of our income in order that good roads may be provided. The provision of transportation might similarly, if we so desire, be made without payment for each act of service. On the other hand, the making of a profit might, if the community wished it, be effected. It would make no difference in considering the cost to the community; it would only affect its incidence. A National Transport Board might so fix its fares that at the end of the year it handed over to the Exchequer a large sum, just as the Post Office does, or it might fix its prices at such a level as to show no profit at all, or even a loss which might be made up from some other source. It would not affect the main issue, which is whether or not the public is provided with the services it requires.

The next objection is that there would not be skilled management. This again is a fallacy. Take the railways as an example. They are managed by boards of directors who are supposed to be elected by a great body of shareholders. These directors are not men skilled in transportation. They appoint men of technical ability to do the actual work. These men would work just as efficiently under a board appointed by the community. The essential change would be one of object. The railway directors to-day have to consider first and foremost the interests of the shareholders. The members of the National Transport Board will only have to consider the interests of the community. There is yet a third objection sometimes put forward on behalf of the technician and the business manager. They fear that in some way they will have less freedom in management than they have to-day; they fear that they will be unduly interfered with. I think that the experience of those who serve the great municipalities or the State in such undertakings as the Post Office shows that there is no substance in this fear. The workers understand very well the function of management, and are not the least likely to interfere unduly. On the contrary, they are far more likely to give support to a manager with progressive ideas than those who look at everything from the narrow point of view of dividends.

Finally there is the objection that there will be a lack of initiative. This assumes that there is already initiative in private enterprise, but only too often this is lacking. The unwillingness of private enterprise to utilise science is well known. There are exceptions, but in general there is a great deal of conservatism in business. The Labour Government will make far greater use of science than is done to-day, because it alone has the policy which will prevent its frustration. Too often scientific advance or business management only results in glutting the market or throwing people out of work, because the economic system is not adapted to take advantage of increased productivity.

SOCIAL AMELIORATION

While it is important that the basic problems of the ownership and control of industry and finance shall be tackled at the outset, Labour does not intend to delay the introduction of measures calculated to effect an immediate improvement of a far-reaching character in the social services. It is determined to put an end once and for all to the insecurity suffered by millions through the fear of unemployment and loss of livelihood. With this end in view, it will start by concentrating available work on those best fitted to perform it. As a first step it intends immediately to raise the school-leaving age to fifteen, and, as soon as the necessary arrangements can be made, to sixteen, with adequate maintenance allowances, and to extend considerably the present facilities for secondary education up to eighteen. In this way the leisure which at present exists in the form of unemployment will be utilised to give every child in the country an opportunity of developing its faculties to the full.

At the other end of the scale, Labour intends to see that all those who have reached an age at which they are entitled to retire from industry shall be given adequate pensions on condition of retirement. Under present conditions, any person retiring from industry has, virtually speaking, to depend on what he has saved in order to spend the rest of his days in anything short of penury. Labour believes that the nation should take proper care of those who have spent their working days in adding to the national wealth, and that they should not simply be thrown upon the scrap-heap after they have ceased to have an economic value.

While taking steps to withdraw from industry all those who ought either to be still at school or to be able to rest after a life spent in industrial employment, a Labour Government will proceed to a drastic reduction of the working hours of those who still remain at work. Modern science has enabled us to produce all that we need with a greatly reduced man-power. The proper distribution of work between all those who are of working age should result in a shorter working week, without reduction of pay, and, indeed, without reduction in production. Both the French and New Zealand Governments have shown that this can be done, with conspicuous success.

A further measure that is long overdue is the enactment of a law giving every worker a statutory fortnight's holiday with pay. This will be one of the Bills that a Labour Government will introduce at an early date. It is, indeed, a ridiculous situation that, while two million people are unemployed, the men and women who are in work should never receive more than a weekend's holiday during the whole of their working life. Here again France and New Zealand have shown us that holidays with pay are feasible.

It is inevitable that during the period of adjustment to the new conditions a certain volume of unemployment should continue. For those who still remain unemployed there must be adequate maintenance. The means test will be abolished, and the whole treatment of the unemployed will be radically altered. Instead of being considered, as they are by the National Government, as something little better than criminals, they will be treated by Labour as the unwilling victims of circumstances over which they have no control.

Labour will not rest, however, until the unemployed have all been absorbed into industry. With this end in view, it will initiate a bold programme of works of public development. Local authorities will be encouraged to embark on activities designed to give this country the best possible housing and educational facilities. This will mean the building of new housing estates, schools, and hospitals, and the provision of work for thousands who to-day are allowed to remain idle while these vitally necessary social services are starved. A programme of electrification will be started, including the electrification of the newly socialised railways. There will, indeed, be an enormous volume of work needed to bring the railways, mines, and other public concerns, which have been taken over from private enterprise, into a condition of full efficiency.

AGRICULTURE

A great opportunity for setting the unemployed to useful and necessary work is to be found in the field of agriculture. Labour proposes to embark on a vigorous programme of agricultural development without delay.

This last year has shown the appalling manner in which agriculture has been neglected by the " National " Government. The first essential of a successful development of British agriculture is that there should be a proper conservation of our natural resources. The farmer cannot work without the equipment necessary to his trade. Yet to-day millions of acres of our land are allowed to lie water-logged, and farms in low-lying areas are even threatened with total destruction by flood, while during the summer months drought has been experienced over large areas of the country. A programme of land drainage will be undertaken immediately, and will continue until every acre of agricultural land is properly drained.

Side by side with this programme, Labour intends to embark on a scheme for land settlement. As the standard of living of the people rises there will naturally be a greatly increased demand for agricultural produce, and as far as is practicable that demand should be met by our own farmers. Groups of smallholders will be established, and especial attention will be paid to the development of forest holdings. At the same time, public farming corporations, capable of farming on a large scale, will be set up. Throughout all this new development, care will be taken to see that the farm worker has, for the first time, an adequate standard of living, and this will be a first charge on the farming industry. In order that people shall be able to buy farm produce at a reasonable price, a full use will be made of Co-operative undertakings and Marketing Boards to narrow the gap between producer and consumer.

THE DISTRESSED AREAS

While paying particular attention to agriculture, however, the Labour Party cannot forget that a special problem exists in the Distressed Areas, and that the solution of this problem must to a large extent be found within the areas themselves. It will not accept the present purely arbitrary boundaries of these areas as defined by law, but will come to the aid of Lancashire and other areas that are at present not placed in the category of what the Government calls "special" areas. There are various ways in which these areas can receive immediate relief. In the first place, it will be necessary to relieve the local authorities in them of a portion of the overwhelming cost of Public Assistance, by means of special Exchequer grants. So long as the burden of Public Assistance in the Special Areas continues to be borne exclusively by the authorities in those areas, the local rates will be out of all proportion to the capacity of the district. This is, however, only a preliminary to a programme of constructive development. Such a programme must include the placing of new industries within the Special Areas. At present the great majority of new industries are established right outside any districts which could possibly be included in the category of Distressed Areas. Only recently we had a peculiarly flagrant case of the misplacement of industry in the Government's proposal to build a new aircraft factory at Maidenhead. Public opinion forced the Government to agree to establish the factory in Lancashire, but the mere fact that it was originally proposed to establish it in the Greater London area shows that the present Government have no conception of the need for bringing industry back to the Distressed Areas. The creation of a National

Investment Board will give the Government power to control in large measure the development of new industries. This power must be used to see that industry develops geographically in accordance with a national plan, and part of that plan will be a rehabilitation of the Distressed Areas. If industry is to be brought to these areas, however, they will have to be made ready to receive it. A considerable amount of "spring cleaning" will be necessary, and the Government will have to make grants to enable this to be done. New facilities will be provided, in the shape of thoroughly efficient and up-to-date housing, schools, and hospitals, while the hideous disorder and devastation which industry has brought in its train, must be, wherever possible, removed. All these plans for the Distressed Areas will be based on the principle that the solution of the problem does not consist in removing people from these areas and transferring them to other parts of the country, but rather in rebuilding industry within the areas themselves. In this way it will be possible to make use of all the existing local services, and above all will be avoided the necessity of breaking up communities which have grown up together, and developed their own local customs and their own way of life.

CHAPTER VIII

FOREIGN POLICY

SOCIALISTS in all countries are united by a common rejection of the doctrines and ideals of militarism and imperialism, and are convinced that the political and economic salvation of mankind lies in the broadest and most generous co-operation. Social justice must be the basis of a peaceful world. The action taken by Socialists in trying to apply their principles necessarily depends on the position of the countries to which they belong.

To understand the attitude of the Labour Party to foreign affairs it is necessary to look back at the past before one considers the present, and to realise what is the background of the average member of the Party. The first thing to remember is that the most prominent feature in that background is the consciousness of Britain's insularity. The age-long immunity from attack of this country has created a habit of mind in the people which is deeply seated. Most people are unaware of the extent to which this historical position affects their outlook even to-day, when the conditions have to such a large extent been altered by the development of air warfare. It requires a real effort of the imagination to grasp these changed circumstances and to get away from the influence of the past. It is necessary to revalue all historical events in the light of modern developments.

This insularity has always made it difficult for British Socialists to understand completely the attitude of their Continental comrades. Continental Socialists are often puzzled by the attitude of British Labour representatives. It accounts also for many of the misunderstandings which have arisen in the ranks of Labour. It is a factor in the mental make-up of the extreme pacifist and of those who demand a stronger attitude in foreign policy.

RETROSPECT

In the years before the war there was little to distinguish the foreign policy of the Labour Party from that of the radical wing of the Liberals. The Party, although comprising within its ranks Socialists, and forming itself part of the Second International, had no real constructive foreign policy, but shared the views which were traditional in radical circles. These were not very coherent. They were based first of all on an individualist conception of the world. A number of sovereign States, following their own conceptions of self-interest, existed in a state of anarchy mitigated by a number of rather vague understandings and rules which were known collectively as international law. The citizens of these States were considered as competing freely with each other in accordance with the best principles of the Manchester school. The ideal aimed at was complete freedom of trade, which was considered to be a satisfactory basis for world peace.

Great Britain was in a peculiarly favoured position owing to her insular situation. She had acquired a large portion of the earth's surface, which was, however, open to the traders of all nations. Her situation made it impossible that she should desire war, and therefore the British Fleet might be regarded rather as a police force in the interests of the world than as a potential menace to other nations. While admitting that in the past Britain has been guilty of aggression, and might be again if imperialism got the upper hand, there was also a feeling that Britain had a special position as a civilising agent, and possessed a specially sensitive conscience in respect to the oppression of the weak by the strong.

The radical tradition was strongly isolationist. It suspected all entanglements with foreign Powers. It was anti-imperialist and anti-militarist. It held that armed forces should be kept at a minimum as potentially dangerous to popular liberties.

There was, however, another radical tradition which looked upon Britain as the champion of liberty against tyranny, and the supporter of all peoples rightly struggling to be free from domestic or foreign oppression. The Palmerstonian tradition of support for Liberal movements abroad was reinforced by the humanitarian impulse which lay behind Gladstone's denunciation of Armenian and Bulgarian atrocities. Thus it was found possible then, as it is to-day, for people to hold strong pacifist views, while claiming the right to denounce oppression all over the world, and to call upon Britain to use her strong arm to protect the weak. The explanation of the paradox lay in the strategic position of Britain. Long immunity from invasion tended to give the pacifists an exaggerated sense of security.

Towards the end of the nineteenth century the imperialism of the Conservative Party which culminated in the Boer War added strength to the radical sentiment. The Boer War showed also the strength of the force of national sentiment which could be aroused in war-time, and the divisions which such a condition would cause in the ranks of Labour. The outbreak of the World War was to reveal this in full measure. The Labour Party had taken its share in the work of the Second International, but Socialists had never worked out a constructive peace policy. The Second International was essentially a gathering together of minorities. It had the minority attitude. Its work was directed to correlating opposition to Governments, not to considering how Socialist Governments would act. This was all too hypothetical. It was assumed that when there were Socialist Governments no difficulties could arise between them. In the meantime, arbitration was pressed as an alternative to war. Much of the propaganda for international arbitration which resulted in the Hague Conference was done by British Socialists and trade unionists, notably Fred Maddison in the early days, while it was Jaurès who first clearly defined the burden of international law by saying, " He who rejects arbitration is the aggressor," the formula later adopted in the Geneva Protocol. The international general strike was considered the most effective sanction for preventing an outbreak. Keir Hardie for years pressed this as a definite policy for the International. The event proved that international solidarity was not strong enough to overcome the force of national sentiment.

THE WORLD WAR

I have not space to consider the actions of Socialists in the various countries in the face of the World War. It is enough for my purpose to indicate one of the reasons for the failure of the workers to act with resolution. The truth is that there never had been worked out a coherent policy. Each party's attitude towards the war was influenced to a very large extent by the degree of democracy in its country, and also by the force of national sentiment, a force often under-estimated by English, though better understood by Scots, Welsh, and Irish. The Russian and the Frenchman could not feel alike because they had Governments of such different composition.

There had been much international sentiment, but little or no consideration of the strategy of the workers. The Labour Party had taken its stand on international brotherhood, and had called for a conference of all nations to bring about agreements for arbitration and the reduction of armaments, but it had not included the essential condition—that is, the supersession of anarchy by the rule of law and the creation of some kind of larger policy. Socialists were not really agreed on policy. There were those who rejected all national feeling, and sought to substitute for it allegiance to an international movement. There were others who thought rather in terms of the workers gaining control of the Governments of their States and collaborating together as national units in a world commonwealth.

The issue which presented itself to Socialists on

the outbreak of the World War was not simple, because the war was not solely one between rival Capitalisms. It was useless for the internationalists to tell the peoples of Central Europe that national differences did not matter. They did matter to them. The force of nationalism was under-estimated by Socialists whose countries had long ago realised their national unity. Further, there was a definite clash between the Capitalist democracies such as France and Britain, and the more authoritarian States such as Germany. They differed just as do to-day the Western democracies and the Fascist States. British Socialists who fought in the war because of the invasion of Belgium were, in their view, standing for the observance of the rule of law in international affairs. Those who declined service either took the extreme pacifist view, which is fundamentally religious and not political, or, holding that there was only one real struggle—that of the workers against the Capitalists—considered there was nothing to choose between the contending States.

AFTER THE WAR

It was remarkable how soon in Britain the deep cleavages of opinion in the Labour movement were reconciled. This was largely due to the fact that in the course of the war it had become plain that some kind of world policy was necessary if civilisation was to survive and the world to be saved from another catastrophe. The conception of the League of Nations was developed in this country very largely under Socialist inspiration. In 1918 the Labour Party, in *Labour and the New Social Order*, demonstrated how far it had progressed in the formation of a constructive policy. It stated, " We stand for the immediate establishment, actually as a part of the Treaty of Peace with which the present war will end, of a universal League or Society of Nations, a supernational authority, with an International High Court to try all justiciable issues between nations; an International Legislature to enact such common laws as can be mutually agreed upon; and an International Council of mediation to endeavour to settle without ultimate conflict even those disputes which are not justiciable. We would have all nations of the world most solemnly undertake and promise to make common cause against any one of them that broke away from this fundamental agreement."

There is no doubt that this lead helped to re-create unity in the Party at home, and to secure international agreement in favour of the League among Socialist Parties at the Conference in 1919.

It was recognised that the League was based on the Peace Treaties, and was an organisation of Capitalist States, but it was welcomed as embodying a conception of a world society. It had behind it a great volume of peace sentiment which the war had created. Thus, when the Labour Party was called upon to take office in 1924 it had a well-considered policy in foreign affairs, based on support of the League and an endeavour to extend its scope. It was realised from the first that the League was only an embryo which, if it were to survive, must develop the necessary organs. The Labour Government took the initiative in proposing the Geneva Protocol. Its object was to strengthen League action by outlawing war, increasing security by making more precise the pledges of joint action against an aggressor, and by providing for the compulsory settlement of all disputes between League members. The Protocol was agreed to by the League Assembly, and at the same time, again on the initiative of the Labour Government, it was decided to summon a world disarmament conference, for disarmament was an integral part of the plan for security under the Protocol.

In two other directions advances towards peace were made; first, in endeavours to get rid of the worst features of the Peace Treaties, and second, in endeavouring to come to an agreement with the U.S.S.R. Unfortunately, the latter attempt was unsuccessful, largely due to the faulty tactics of the rulers of the U.S.S.R. The

Labour Government fell, and the Conservatives refused to ratify the Protocol. Subsequent events have shown that Labour's policy was right. For five vital years there was a Conservative Government in power in Great Britain, and the favourable time for building peace on firm foundations, for strengthening the League and obtaining substantial disarmament, was allowed to pass away.

It was not until 1929 that Labour obtained a further opportunity of putting into practice its foreign policy. This time it met with far greater success. Mr. Arthur Henderson entered the Foreign Office with a perfectly clear idea of what he wanted to do and how to do it. During his two years of office the overwhelming majority of the member States of the League signed the optional clause of the Statute of the Permanent Court of International Justice on the initiative of the British Government. Thus the old objective of the Labour Party, the substitution of compulsory arbitration in place of war, was realised, and the world had taken a big step forward on the road from anarchy to international government.

A real attempt was made to get rid of the most onerous clauses of the Peace Treaties, notably by securing the withdrawal of the troops from the Rhine. The most important step of all, however, was the summoning of the long delayed Disarmament Conference. The Labour Government, however, fell before the fruit of Mr. Henderson's work could be gathered. It left office having raised Great Britain to the leadership of the peace movement and having brought about conditions most favourable for a real advance to world appeasement.

During the first years of the National Government the Disarmament Conference met, and there still seemed to be a possibility that something effective might be done, although the failure by the British representatives to give a strong lead indicated the likelihood that the essentially reactionary character of the Government would show itself at Geneva and lead to failure and futility.

Meanwhile in the Labour movement opinion had steadily developed in support of the policy of full support for the League.

The history of the last five years in international politics has been marked by the failure of the leading countries to carry out the principles of the League Covenant, the rise of dictatorships based on force, the growth of armaments, and a steady drift towards another world war. The failure to stop Japanese aggression in the Far East encouraged all those who put their trust in armaments. The failure of the Disarmament Conference and the blundering in dealing with the German republican Government led to the

Op

success of Hitlerism in Germany. The next step was the betrayal of Abyssinia, and finally the acquiescence in the Fascist support for General Franco in Spain. Every event has marked a stage in the degeneration of the international situation. Behind these political events lay the world economic crisis which created the conditions which made them possible.

The Labour Party, in supporting throughout a strict adherence to the principles of the League of Nations, pointed the course which would have averted the dangers which the world is now facing.

At Hastings, Southport, and Brighton the Annual Conferences of the Party confirmed the policy of support of the League, but, distrustful of Capitalist Governments, it adopted at Hastings a resolution calling upon the National Executive to seek consultation forthwith with the Trade Union and Co-operative movements with a view to deciding and announcing to the country what steps, including a general strike, were to be taken to organise the opposition of the working-class movement in the event of war or threat of war.

There was nothing inconsistent in this resolution with the policy of the Party in supporting the League of Nations. Labour Party policy has been summed up by Mr. Henderson as world-peace loyalty. This comprises arbitration insistence, the duty to insist that our Government settle all its disputes by peaceful means; sanctions assistance, the duty of supporting collective action; and war resistance, the refusal to support our own Government if it were the aggressor or refused arbitration and became involved in war. The general strike is in this connection a sanction to be used against a Government which has itself become a law-breaker.

In 1934, at the Southport Conference, the Party adopted a comprehensive statement, under the heading " War and Peace," which set out in full the principles for which the Party stands and the policy which it would pursue when given power. It stands to-day as the official policy of the Party. Its principal points were these: it based Labour's foreign policy on the collective peace system through the League of Nations, but, so far from regarding the League as only an adjunct to foreign policy and the collective system as a collateral security to national armaments, it regarded the League as a first step towards a co-operative world commonwealth. It rejected the theory of the balance of power and demanded the subordination of national sovereignty to world obligations. It stressed the need for basing the new world order on social justice and demanded far-reaching measures of economic co-operation and world control in economic and financial matters, such as raw materials, transport, travel and communications, hours and conditions of labour, etc. It linked disarmament with collective security, and accepted the obligation to use armed force if necessary in restraining an aggressor State. It declared for an international police force. It stressed the need for world loyalty as against national loyalty. It regarded war resistance as the duty of every citizen, and not merely of organised Labour.

The test of the full acceptance of this policy came when Italy committed aggression against Abyssinia and the League of Nations decided to impose sanctions. In the circumstances the Labour Party had no option but to stand firm by its principles and support League action, although it realised very fully the danger that its attitude might be exploited by its opponents. This fear proved to be well grounded, for it has now been authoritatively explained that the decision of the National Government to support the Covenant was based upon a consideration of electoral chances. Support of collective security was only a means in order to obtain a majority for a Government which intended to use its power for building up great national armaments. The Government abandoned Abyssinia and the defence of collective security with complete cynicism, in spite of the specific pledges of the speeches made in Geneva by Sir Samuel Hoare and Mr. Eden, and the promise made on the eve of the General Election of 1935 that " in the present unhappy dispute between Italy and Abyssinia there will be no wavering in the policy hitherto pursued."

The Abyssinian question was the cause of a cleavage of opinion in the ranks of Labour. While the great majority of the Party stood by the policy which had been approved by Conference, those who took the extreme pacifist point of view were not prepared to take any action which might lead to war, while a small section held the view that as long as there was a Capitalist Government in this country it must be opposed, even if it was professedly acting with the League of Nations. This view was held despite the fact that the U.S.S.R. had become a member of the League.

THE PRESENT OUTLOOK

During the last two years the position of the League of Nations has still further deteriorated. The world situation has become far more dangerous than when the Labour Party's policy was elaborated. There are some who ask whether it has any validity to-day, when the League of Nations has been so seriously weakened, and when the menace of the aggressive Fascist Powers has become so great. It is, therefore, necessary to re-examine the policy of the Party in the light of the facts of the existing situation.

First of all, it is right to stress the large measure

of agreement in the Party before considering the points of divergence. The Party is agreed in its rejection of the policy of the balance of power and of the use of force as an instrument of policy. It is agreed on the objective of a World Co-operative Commonwealth. It aims at the subordination of national sovereignty to world loyalty, the reduction of all national armaments to the lowest possible level by international agreement, and to the substitution of arbitration for war. All agree on the need for removing private profit in the manufacture of and trade in arms. Equally, there is no difference of opinion as to the vital necessity of removing the economic causes of war and of basing the new world order on firm economic foundations as well as on political institutions. The differences of opinion arise over two questions—the use of force and the extent of the possible co-operation with Capitalist States or with non-Socialists.

All Socialists are profoundly opposed to war, and those who regard the use of force as necessary do not regard it as desirable, but only as an unavoidable necessity at our present stage of society. There are, however, a number of members of the Party who for one reason or another take up the line of absolute opposition to any use of armed force. For the sake of brevity I will call these the pacifists.

The pacifists fall into two groups: the optimists

and the pessimists. The optimists believe that force can never accomplish anything good, and that it is, in effect, unnecessary, because right is might and will prevail. Wrong can never conquer in the long run. They believe in complete disarmament, and consider all war, for whatever reason it is waged, as a crime. The Party has always contained men and women who take this attitude, and has conceded to them a very full measure of liberty of action, for it is recognised that this is a case where the individual conscience rules. It cannot be denied that this wide tolerance has at times been the cause of some confusion in the Party.

I have the greatest respect for those who hold this view, but I cannot accept its validity. I do not think that the main thesis is proven. It is not a doctrine that is really compatible with political action if carried to its logical conclusion, for all government rests ultimately on the sanction of force, although it may be held in the background. Pushed to its logical conclusion, non-resistance is the negation of government, and leads straight to anarchy. Actually those who take this line do not press the doctrine very far. They will invoke force in order to remedy social evils, to make a landlord repair his slum property, and to compel a sweater to pay fair wages. They support a police force but reject an army. To my mind this is illogical. The amount of force necessary to enforce the will of the community is conditioned by the forces that are in opposition. It is possible to make a slum landlord put his house in repair without physical violence, because the offender has no armed force to bring against the State. In this country the police keep order without arms because offenders are as a rule unarmed, but it is not so in every country. Elsewhere, the preservation of the liberties of the citizens often involves exposing to the risk of death the members of the police force. Whether the amount of force used is great or small, the principle involved is the same. If there is a law, and if that law is to be supported by the sanction of force, the sanction must be adequate in order to be successful. Those who oppose the pacifist view cannot admit that there is no difference between the use of force in support of law and its use for individual advantage. The one is police action, the other war. No system of international co-operation can endure unless it is founded on a basis of law which is upheld with the same vigour and success as is the law of a national State. A good deal of British pacifism is the result rather of the conditions obtaining in this country than of firmly held doctrine. With those who sincerely hold the doctrine of non-resistance in its absolute form it is useless to argue; one can but disagree.

The pessimistic pacifists do not take the ground of a moral objection to the use of force, but hold that the horrors of war are so great, and the possible gains from it so small, that at any cost it must be avoided as the greatest of all evils. It is, in their view, necessary to submit to the will of the evildoers, lest a worst thing come upon us. It is undeniable that there is much to be said for this point of view at the present time, when science applied to the weapons of destruction seems to have made defence of any kind almost hopeless, and when the probable results of another war are so terrible. Its acceptance seems to me to involve complete surrender to the evildoer. It means that society definitely says to the anti-social, " Do what you please." I am not prepared to accept that position. I recognise the great dangers, which are not merely those of war itself, but the danger of being conquered spiritually by the very forces which are to be resisted. If the forces of tyranny are prepared to take risks, and know that the forces of liberty are not, liberty will not long survive.

The second body of objectors to the policy of the Labour Party are the class-war enthusiasts. They are the antithesis of the pacifists. They hold that Socialism will only be won by force, and that a war between the rival ideologies of Capitalism, in its modern form of Fascism, and Communism is inevitable sooner or later. It is a logical position to take up. For reasons which I have already stated I do not believe that the class-struggle must be fought out with violence in this country, nor do I believe that a world war between Capitalism and Socialism is inevitable. I agree, indeed, with the pacifists in holding that another world war would be a disaster to civilisation; the object of all our policy must, therefore, be to prevent " the next war " from breaking out, rather than to win it when it comes; and for this the only hope lies in collective security founded on law.

A less extreme view is that taken by those who hold that all action within a country must be considered in terms of the class war. They deny that there is any possibility of common interest between the workers and other sections of the community. In effect, they deny the possibility of national action. I think that this view is false, and that it does not correspond with the facts. Among those facts is the state of mind of the workers themselves. It is no use telling the ordinary Briton that it does not matter to him whether he is ruled by British or foreign capitalists. He does not believe it. He is right. The condition of the citizen of Britain is very different from that of the German or the Italian. There are things which the Briton has which he values and is not prepared to surrender without a struggle. There is a wide difference between Capitalist Democracy and the Corporate State. While it is true that there is a contest between those who own and those who labour, it is not as clear-cut as some theorists would maintain. There are in this country very many gradations between the proletarian and the absolute *rentier*. It is an over-simplification of the problem which has to be faced to reduce everything to the terms of the class-struggle.

The logic of this attitude is that there can never be action by the country as a whole. If a Capitalist Government is in power, the workers must resist everything that the Government does. If a Socialist Government is in power, the Capitalists will do the same. The result is that the country ceases to count as a factor in world affairs. It is immobilised until the class-struggle has been resolved.

The alternative policy is not the support by Labour of a Capitalist Government, but constitutional opposition. The Labour Party opposes Government policy, and seeks to convert the country to its point of view, but it does not carry on a campaign of resistance, passive or active, to hinder the ordinary functions of Government being carried on. It accepts the will of the majority, which has decided that the country shall be governed by a Capitalist Government, and it expects its opponents to do the same when it is returned to power. The Labour Party does, however, take the line that where the Government is disregarding its obligations under the League of Nations, and is acting aggressively, it is the duty of all those who support League loyalty as against national loyalty to oppose the Government by every means in its power.

There is yet one other tendency among Labour supporters. There are those who, realising the danger of the menace of the Fascist Powers, tend to take up an attitude of supporting a Capitalist Government at home as the least of two evils. They tend to under-estimate the reality of the struggle between Capitalism and Socialism and to magnify the differences between democratic Capitalist States and Fascist States. The danger of this attitude is that in fighting foreign Fascism they may encourage the subtle introduction of Fascism at home. The Fascist danger in this country does not come from the crude activities of Sir Oswald Mosley, but from the clever propaganda which has been actively disseminated ever since the formation of the National Government in favour of what is called national unity. There has been a deliberate attempt made to suggest that after all there are no real political differences in this country, and that everybody is in reality in agreement. The increasing danger of the international situation affords an opportunity for pressing this point. The speeches of Mr. Ramsay MacDonald are full of Fascist ideas and even Fascist phraseology. The essentials of the Corporate State without any coloured shirts might be introduced in this country in a period of international tension.

I have set out these divergent views, not in order to emphasise disunity, because the great majority of the Party do not share them, but rather in order to bring out the issues which have to be faced.

THE PRESENT SITUATION

I believe that the general principles of Labour's foreign policy are absolutely right, and that it is only by putting them into practical operation that war can be avoided and a stable peace be assured. The question which really arises is as to their particular application to the existing situation. We must consider what that is.

In Europe to-day there are a number of democratic States in the west: Great Britain, France, Holland, Belgium, and the four Scandinavian countries. In many of these, including France, Socialists are collaborating in their Governments. In Great Britain and Holland there are strong Labour movements in opposition to Capitalist Governments which profess the principles of democracy. In Czecho-Slovakia there is also a democratic Government in which Socialists share responsibility. Switzerland, standing apart from all other groups, is the only other fully democratic State, though there is a measure of democracy in a number of other countries which are not yet wholly Fascist, such as the Balkan States.

The U.S.S.R., the only State under Communist rule, is a member of the League, and in foreign affairs has taken a very realistic line. Instead of the attitude of indiscriminate hostility to all Capitalist Governments, it draws a distinction between those which are definitely pacific and those which are potentially aggressive.

There are, on the other side, the two aggressive Fascist States, one inside and one outside the League, Italy and Germany, which pursue a policy based on force. Outside Europe, and also outside the League, is a third aggressive State, Japan. When republican Spain has won her fight there should be another democracy to be added on the side of the League.

The other European States are ruled by Governments of varying degrees of dictatorship, while the States outside Europe which are members of the League are not in a position, by reason of their weakness and geographical position, to play an active part in solving the problems of Europe, though their joint action in the political and economic field may be very valuable.

The League has suffered severely in prestige by the failure over the Abyssinian affair, and is, in fact, challenged by the Fascist States. The collective peace system is not a reality at the present time. Instead, there are a series of groupings within the League, such as the Little Entente and the Franco-British Entente, which is in fact, if not in form, almost a defensive alliance, and the Franco-Soviet Pact, which is more definitely one. It is not possible to draw a hard and fast line between all the States of Europe and assign them to a definite sphere of influence. If this were so, we should be very near the position which existed before the World War, when there were rival camps in Europe and a number of States whose adherence to either side was doubtful. In fact, there is at the present time no such absolute alliance between the Fascist States, nor is there any real agreement between those who are opposed to them.

What there is at the present time is a state of unstable equilibrium in a Europe where armaments are being rapidly increased. There is any amount of inflammable material scattered about, and the chances of ignition are very great. The possibilities of stopping the flame from spreading are less than formerly, owing to the rapidity with which modern warfare can be initiated. A disturbing feature of the situation is the development of a new technique of aggression which is now being exemplified in Spain, whereby interference in the internal affairs of another country constitutes aggression on the part of those interfering.

If the Labour Party came into power now in

this country there would not, I think, be any division of opinion as to what policy should be followed. A Labour Government would at once take action to rebuild the League of Nations and the collective system, but it would regard the League not as a collateral security for national defence; it would endeavour to build up the strength of the League so that it should become a closely knit organisation able to stand against an aggressor. A Labour Government would be prepared to do its part in a real system of collective security. On the other hand, it would not be content with a League which merely stabilised the existing conditions in the world. Collective security is essential in order that the real work of dealing with the causes of war should be taken in hand. I do not believe that a war of ideologies is inevitable. I believe that the way to meet Fascism is not by force of arms, but by showing that with co-operation in the economic sphere far better conditions are obtainable than by pursuing a policy of aggression. The League should be used, not as the framework of an alliance of States united against those outside it, but as an organisation within which there are the widest opportunities for all States, a League open to all States which will come in and accept its conditions. If the Fascist States prefer to remain outside, they must of course do so, and the League must maintain forces strong enough to resist any attempt at aggression. If economic solidarity were added to political union in the League, I believe that the conditions of the States inside the League would be so immeasurably better than those obtaining in the States outside it that the latter would sooner or later be drawn in. If Labour were in power in this country, it could, with France and the U.S.S.R. and the smaller States which are largely governed under Socialist inspiration, pursue a policy of international economic co-operation based upon the utilisation of abundance instead of restriction, which would rapidly have its effect on world economic conditions. A programme of economic development under League auspices would do much to remove the conditions which lead to war and dictatorship. With such immense economic resources within the League properly utilised, a great raising of the standard of life throughout the world would be possible, provided that the internal organisation within the States permitted mass consumption to match with the increase of production. Under such conditions of co-operation an all-round reduction of armaments would be possible. Labour's peace policy would be constructive—the building up of a world economic commonwealth of nations co-operating together but retaining their own distinctive polities and abstaining from interfering with each others' internal affairs.

But at the present time Labour is not in power. It is in opposition to a Capitalist Government which, while professing devotion to the League of Nations, has shown itself completely untrustworthy. What is to be the attitude of the Labour Party in opposition? First it must be perfectly clear that the Labour Party rejects altogether the theory that foreign policy is something which must be kept out of party politics. It does not agree that there is some policy to be pursued by this country irrespective of what party is in power, a policy which is national and so transcends party differences. There is a deep difference of opinion between the Labour Party and the Capitalist parties on foreign as well as on home policy, because the two cannot be separated. The foreign policy of a Government is the reflection of its internal policy. Imperialism is the form which Capitalism takes in relation to other nations. A Capitalist Government in Britain thinks of the League of Nations as a means of preserving peace, because peace is a British interest, but still more it thinks of it as a means of preserving the British Empire and British Imperial interests. It does not consider it as a world commonwealth in embryo, because its outlook is nationalist not internationalist. It may on particular occasions take action in foreign affairs with which the Labour Party agrees, because for the time being the supposed interests of

Britain coincide with the general interests of the world. It is, therefore, stupid to suggest, as some people do, that a general guide to international politics is to oppose everything the British Capitalist Government does, but such particular instances of action which can be approved by Socialists do not affect the truth of the general proposition that there is no agreement on foreign policy between a Labour Opposition and a Capitalist Government.

CHAPTER IX

THE COMMONWEALTH AND THE EMPIRE

THE TASK which faces the Labour Party in Britain, as in other imperialist countries, is more complicated than that which has to be dealt with by Socialists in those States with little or no possessions overseas. While, on the one hand, it is the protagonist at home of the struggle of the workers against the Capitalists, it is, in relation to the less developed peoples of the world, part of a dominant race which collectively exploits them. As long as the Socialist movement was only a propagandist body, with no prospect of achieving power, it was possible to take up a purely negative and critical attitude. Imperialism was seen to be an extension into a wider sphere of the Capitalism which had to be opposed at home. Socialists took their full share in denouncing and exposing the exploitation of the black, brown, and yellow races, which was invested with so much glamour by Joseph Chamberlain and the apostles of the idea of Empire. As, however, the crude imperialism of early days became modified, largely through the force of public opinion created by the efforts of radicals, Socialists, and humanitarians, it was realised that the relationship between advanced and backward peoples raised problems not easy of solution. The past could not be wiped out. Simple surrender of all ill-gotten gains was undesirable and unpractical. The Labour Party has, therefore, given much time to the consideration of colonial problems and to the application of Socialist principles in this sphere.

The British Labour Party, however, unlike other European Socialist Parties, finds itself faced also with the problems which arise from the fact that Britain is a member of the British Commonwealth of Nations. The Labour Party has always steadily supported the furthering of the process whereby the colonies of the past have developed into the Dominions of to-day, equal in status to the mother country. The Statute of Westminster marked the end of the old conception of a colonial empire of white settlers subordinate to the power and subservient to the interests of a European State. But the conceding of full equality of status does not solve all the problems to which this association gives rise. Questions of foreign policy, defence, migration, and trade require careful examination. The very lack of definition in the Commonwealth Constitution, and the fact that it is in effect a federation without a federal authority, raises difficult problems which sooner or later must be solved if the Commonwealth is to continue. The relationship between the Commonwealth and the League of Nations, and the obligations imposed by membership of both bodies, require considerable elucidation.

It is, therefore, necessary to try to set out the Labour Party position both to the Commonwealth and to the Empire.

IMPERIALISM

The Labour Party is, of course, opposed to imperialism, whether in its old or its new form. In its old form it was based definitely on the conception of overseas possessions as being primarily designed for the profit and prestige of the imperial Power. The loss of the American colonies modified to some extent this conception by introducing as a matter of necessity some attention to the rights and interests of the inhabitants of overseas territories. Free Trade principles applied in the nineteenth century opened the British Empire to traders of all nations, while the grant of self-government to those colonies inhabited by people of European extraction led eventually to the adoption by them of Tariff policies directed not only against foreigners, but against the home country and other Dominions.

COMMONWEALTH AND THE EMPIRE 231

The continued existence of the British Empire unattacked for so many years was due to its being a Free Trade area so far as its non-self-governing units were concerned. The imperialism of Joseph Chamberlain sought to bind the Empire together by economic ties. The Ottawa agreements marked the triumph, after many years of agitation, of this policy. It brought to an end the conditions under which it had been possible for the British Empire to continue to contain within itself a quarter of the world's population and a quarter of its area without provoking violent opposition from the rest of the world.

The British Empire was built up on sea power. The favourable position of the British Isles, divorced to a large extent from Continental quarrels, enabled this great Empire to be established and to be exploited by British capital made available by the exploitation of the workers at home. The workers had to find the blood and treasure by which it was acquired and maintained. In the conditions of the modern world I do not think that the Empire could be defended against a serious attack made by an alliance of those countries which feel themselves excluded from a share of so large a part of the world. The British Empire can only continue by the goodwill of the rest of the world and by co-operating with other nations in developing the resources of the world in the interest of all peoples. I do not believe that the Dominions themselves would be prepared to follow a policy of exclusiveness in which an endeavour was made to create out of the British Empire and Commonwealth an economic unit. Apart from sentiment and prestige, which are very powerful with the adherents of the imperial idea, the real interest is that of British Capitalists. Here there arise many difficulties. Of recent years we have seen the struggle between those Capitalists and landlords whose interests lie in the rent and profit derived from Great Britain and those who have invested their money in the Dominions, and the conflicting claims of investors in the Empire and in the Argentine.

The great difficulty in consolidating the British Commonwealth is that it is essentially a moneylenders' empire. The crisis of 1931 was very largely due to the fact that owing to the fall in the prices of primary products the moneylenders could not get their interest, while, owing to the working of the Capitalist system on which they depended, the workers of the old world could not effectively consume the products of the new.

The imperialism of the Conservative Party, so far from preserving the British Empire and the Commonwealth, is calculated to lose the one and break up the other. It is one of the curiosities of politics that the Conservative Party should consider itself as the special champion of the

Empire. Conservatism estranged Ireland, would have lost South Africa but for its removal from power at a critical time, and may yet lose India. Its economic basis makes it impossible for it to effect full co-operation with the self-governing Dominions, for the means test and all it stands for are the negation of the utilisation of abundance which is necessary for the development of the countries which produce primary products.

THE LABOUR PARTY AND THE COMMONWEALTH

As I have indicated, the British Empire considered as a political unit consists of two sections. The first is composed of those countries which are free and equal partners in the Commonwealth, enjoying complete self-government and remaining within the Empire of their own free will, while the second, which is, from the point of view of population, by far the largest, contains a number of countries which are in various stages of development towards self-government, and some which are still directly ruled by representatives of this country. The Dominions of Canada, Australia, and New Zealand, with the Irish Free State, are almost entirely inhabited by people of European stock, and with Great Britain form an ideal basis for the development of an economic and political federation that may show an example of how such a relationship can be extended to cover all those countries which are ready to share in collective security and the pooling of economic resources. South Africa, which has not a predominantly white population, offers some problems which must be considered separately, but also forms part of this group.

The Labour Party believes in the closest possible co-operation between these countries, not in order to build up an exclusive block against the rest of the world, but to show the way of advance to the world. All these countries are democratic, and share a common heritage and to a large extent a common language and culture. While each country would remain free and independent, they would take concerted action for the common good of all their peoples. Now that the last remnants of domination have been removed and complete sovereignty attained, the way is open for beginning that process of surrendering absolute sovereignty to a larger unity which is essential if a world commonwealth is to be established. It is in the economic field that this co-operation can be effected first. Some idea of the manner in which inter-trading might be developed in accordance with Socialist conceptions has been afforded by the visit of the Finance Minister of New Zealand to this country. The Labour Government in that Dominion is building up a Socialist economy. The Government has taken control of the entire export trade in dairy products. All such products leave the country to-day as the property of the Government, and most of them find their way to the British market. When they reach London, however, there is no complementary system by which they can be purchased by a body representing the consumers except in so far as they are bought by the Co-operative Wholesale Societies. They enter into the field of Capitalist competition, and, before they reach the consumer, have to pay toll to numerous middlemen. A Socialist Government in this country with a system of Import Boards acting in close collaboration with the consumers' organisations, could contract direct with the New Zealand Government for its supplies. It could, through a system of Export Boards, arrange for sending the goods which go to pay for these imports. It could, if in control of the financial system, arrange more easily for credits. This is but one instance, but it shows what might be done.

At the time of writing the Imperial Conference is sitting. Whatever it may attempt to achieve, it will be hampered by the fact that participating Governments are unable to build up any rational and planned system of inter-Dominion trade as long as they are in the hands of private interests. This was illustrated very clearly at the Ottawa Conference. A great beginning could be made in planning the production and allocation of raw materials and foodstuffs from which might be developed eventually a world planning of economic resources. Equally important from the point of view of the Dominions would be the fact that a Labour Government would plan this country in such a way as to ensure that every man, woman, and child was adequately fed as a prime duty of the State. There would thus be available the greatest possible effective demand for those products which especially concern the Dominions.

Such trading arrangements would of course have to be undertaken with a full realisation that Britain is not the only market for Dominion products, and that the Dominions are not the only producers. I have previously indicated the need for the development of an economic organ of the League of Nations. The agreements made between the units of the British Commonwealth could be fitted into the general world planning which must ultimately be achieved.

DEFENCE

The Dominions are represented in the League of Nations as sovereign States. Their respective geographical positions necessarily affect their attitudes to the problem of collective security. I believe that they should make their contribution within the League rather than through the

Empire apart from the League. Not the least of the many evil results of the National Government's action over the Abyssinian question was the weakening of the faith of the Dominions in the League of Nations and in the word of the British Government. I do not believe that, should another war break out, the Dominions would again give their services as they did in 1914 unless our participation in that war was beyond all question in support of the League and in restraint of an aggressor. Without the unifying factor of the League the Dominions will more and more tend to follow courses of action which seem to make for their immediate interests and to adopt towards Europe and its concerns the attitude of the United States. From the point of view of world peace it is most desirable that these democracies, with their detachment from old European quarrels, should carry full weight in the discussions at Geneva. It is through collective security under the League that it will be possible to arrive at the contribution which each constituent of the Commonwealth should make to the common defence.

SOUTH AFRICA

It is obvious that in the case of the Dominions, there is no question of the oppression of a subject race by Great Britain, but there is the exceptional position in the Union of South Africa. Here there is a majority of primitive peoples ruled over by a white minority. The problems which arise are similar to those which I discuss later in regard to the Colonial Empire, but the responsibility for settling them is not now ours. We have handed them over to the Union Government. The policy pursued by the Dominion Government must, however, have far-reaching effects on the position of Great Britain in Africa. There should be throughout the British Empire a common attitude towards native problems, and a serious divergence from it by one of the Dominions may quite possibly jeopardise the good relations between white and black in other areas.

THE COLONIAL EMPIRE

In the Dominions we have seen a steady progress to complete self-government. It is the aim of the Labour Party to see its extension throughout all the territories of the Empire. At the present time there are two instances, Newfoundland and Malta, where there has been, for different reasons, retrogression. In India and Burma, which I shall deal with later, there has been advance. Over the rest of the Empire there is a great variety of government, with different degrees of participation by the people.

The history of colonial expansion is a terrible

record of cruelty to, and exploitation of, backward peoples by the advanced races. Great Britain must take her full share of blame. There has, however, been during the last half-century a great advance in colonial administration, due primarily to the agitation of philanthropic and religious bodies and radical and Socialist politicians at home, but also to the enlightened work of administrators such as Frederick Lugard. But for this work the conception of trusteeship and the Dual Mandate would in all probability never have developed. The Labour Party has taken its full share in all these endeavours. It realises, however, that the problems of colonial administration are very varied, and that it is impossible to lay down some hard and fast system to fit every case. It has, however, worked out the principles which it would apply as an alternative to imperialism.

Whatever may have been the history of the acquisition of the British Colonial Empire, the fact remains that Great Britain is responsible for the welfare of millions of coloured peoples. It is not possible simply to relinquish control, for the impact of European civilisation has been felt by all native communities, generally with a disintegrating effect upon the structure of native society. The task of adapting these communities to Western conceptions, while preserving all that is best in their own civilisations, is one that presents immense difficulties, but which must inevitably be tackled if the retention of these territories by Great Britain is to be justified. There are two dangers. One is that under the guise of introducing civilisation the native worker will merely be exploited by the European Capitalist; the other that under the pretence of preserving native institutions the natives may be kept ignorant and subordinate.

The Labour Party's objectives have been summed up in two words: " socialisation " and " self-government." The exact form which self-government will take must be decided in each case, for there is a grave objection to trying to transplant institutions which are indigenous to Britain into a soil in which they cannot flourish. There are colonies which are already ripe for a greater degree of autonomy than they now possess. A Labour Government would always prefer to err in being too soon rather than too late in the grant of self-government. There is an inevitable tendency, even in the best of colonial administrators, to lay too much stress on the deterioration in administrative standards which is almost certain to ensue, and not enough on the need for enabling backward peoples to learn to govern themselves.

There is a false demand for " self-government " which comes from ruling British minorities, which seek to escape from the impact of public opinion

COMMONWEALTH AND THE EMPIRE 241

at home and to realise their ambition of governing the native population themselves. The Labour Party will always insist on the widest franchise being given, for exploitation by one set of oppressors may easily be exchanged only for that of another unless care is taken to see that the constitution is really democratic.

Over a large area the peoples are not ready yet for self-government, and in these territories the Labour Party considers that the British Government must act as trustee for the native races. In order to give full effect to the principle of trusteeship the British Government should accept the mandatory principle for all British colonial possessions. This will mean that it will accept regular examination by the League of Nations into its administration of all territories which are inhabited by backward races and are not self-governing, in the same way as Mandatory Powers accept it to-day for their mandated territories. It would necessarily follow from this that there would be an open door for all nations and an abandonment of the attempt to extend the principles of the Ottawa agreements. The extension of the mandatory principle would have other far-reaching effects. The defence of mandated territories concerns the League of Nations and not merely the Mandatory Power. The constant endeavour of the Conservative Party to draw a distinction between imperial defence and collective security would be defeated. The development of common standards in relation to the treatment of backward peoples by European nations would be immensely facilitated. In time there might develop an international civil service all over the world, drawn from the nationals of many countries but inspired by a common ideal: the raising of the standard of life and culture of the less advanced races.

The main problems that affect in varying degrees every one of the British colonies relate to land, labour, taxation, and education. In many of them British settlers have appropriated the most fertile territories and driven the original inhabitants into inferior regions. It has been maintained that the natives cannot develop their land properly themselves, and that the most economical way to run the colony is for Europeans to own the land and for the natives to work for them. This is the policy that has been pushed to its furthest extremes in East Africa. It is, of course, a perfectly natural form of economy under Capitalism. The results have entirely failed to prove the thesis. Production in East Africa is considerably below that in West Africa, where native rights in the land have been preserved. The Labour Party will see that every native family is assured of sufficient land for its support, and will regard all land in the colonies as primarily held in trust for the native inhabitants.

The land question is closely bound up with that of the supply of labour; indeed, the deprivation of the native of his rights in the land has been effected largely in order that he might be compelled to sell his labour cheaply to the white Capitalist. For a similar reason taxation has been imposed, the money for which can only be obtained by wage-earning. The Labour Party will terminate these devices, and will impose taxation only for revenue purposes. The proper control of the migration of labour and of labour conditions will be considered primarily from the point of view of their effect on the native people, and not of company profits.

The organisation of the marketing of native products will be undertaken in order that the producers may obtain a proper return for their labour. This is not possible as long as particular products are monopolised by Capitalist combines.

The Labour Party believes, however, that the key to native development lies in education. The prejudice against the "educated native," which is often expressed in the statement that education and missions destroy the character of the native, is due to the fact that the educated native can stand up to oppression better than his ignorant fellows, and so is inconvenient to the exploiter. The aim of Labour's policy will be to fit the natives to control their own affairs and to achieve self-government.

I have already stated that it is the intention of the Labour Party to reject altogether the conception of a Colonial Empire as an exclusive field of exploitation for the British Capitalist. The issue which this raises is of great importance in considering the causes of unrest which make for war. The demand of Germany and other countries for colonial possessions is being put forward with increasing vigour. The grounds of this demand will not stand examination. The point of prestige belongs to a conception of world politics which is foreign to the Labour conception of a world Commonwealth of Nations, and is indeed even antagonistic to the principles of the League of Nations. The demand for colonies on the ground that without them an advanced industrial country is denied access to raw materials, and is obliged to accept a low standard of life, is disproved by the facts. Germany's difficulty in obtaining raw materials is due to her own financial and economic policy. The standard of life in countries such as Sweden and Denmark, without colonies, is as high as, or higher than, that in France and Belgium, despite their great empires.

It is, however, difficult without an appearance of hypocrisy for Great Britain to make these replies sound convincing. The Labour Party does not believe in a re-allocation of colonial territories between the various great Powers. That is no solution to the problem. The way to deal with these alleged grievances is by rejecting altogether the concepts of imperialism, and by establishing through the League of Nations international control of raw materials. It is obvious that the Labour Party will oppose the handing over of any native peoples to the tender mercies of a Government which is intoxicated with ideas of race superiority, and which has shown a complete inability to deal justly with minorities.

INDIA

There remain to be considered those countries which, possessing civilisations of their own, have yet been for many generations under the control of Great Britain. The outstanding example is India. The Labour Party has always fully accepted the right of the Indian peoples to govern themselves, but it has recognised that the problem involved in developing self-governing institutions in a great continent inhabited by peoples who differ in language, race, and creed is no easy one. The long period of British rule has created a situation in which there have been many rights acquired by particular sections of the Indian people. It is not right to abandon control without taking care to see that these rights will be respected. " India for the Indians " is a simple slogan, but it is necessary to see what it means in terms of human life. There is no particular gain in handing over the peasants and workers of India to be exploited by their own Capitalists and landlords. Nationalism is a creed that may be sustained with great self-sacrifice and idealism, but may shelter class domination and intolerance of minorities as well as economic exploitation.

Throughout all the enquiries into the constitutional position of India, and also of Burma, Labour members have always realised that nationalism was not enough. They have always sought to give to the Indian masses the potential power of bettering their economic conditions by political action. They have recognised frankly that it is unlikely that a poor and illiterate population will escape exploitation at the hands of the rich, the privileged, and the educated classes, but they have stood firm for giving them the possibility of advance. They have recognised also that it is impossible for an alien race to overcome the social and economic evils which are closely bound up with the whole conceptions of the Indian people. Only the Indian people themselves can work out their salvation. The sooner they have the full opportunity to do so the better. The same considerations apply to the much easier case of Burma and to some other parts of the British Empire.

To conclude, the Labour Party, having to deal

with the actual existence of the British Empire and Commonwealth, will seek to apply in that sphere, as in all others, the principles of Socialism. The fact that over a huge area of the earth's surface there is a common sovereignty is advantageous, provided this unity is but a step in a greater unity. One of the vital questions for the future of world peace is the reconciliation of the interests of the white, the black, the brown, and the yellow races. The Labour Party fearlessly applies to this problem the principle of the brotherhood of man. It does not admit that the white race has any right of primogeniture in the world. It holds that the resources of the world must be developed in the interests of all people, and that the standard of life of the inhabitants of Asia and Africa must be raised, and not kept always below those of Europe, America, and Australia.

CHAPTER X

LABOUR AND DEFENCE

I HAVE IN THE PREVIOUS CHAPTER dealt with the attitude of the Labour Party towards foreign affairs, and have discussed the position of the pacifist. I have shown that the Labour Party, while holding as an ideal to be reached some day the complete abolition of all armed forces, is not in favour of a policy of disarmament by example. It does not believe that for this country to abolish all its armed forces would be an effective contribution to world peace.

While admitting the necessity in the present state of the world for this country to make its contribution to the armed forces necessary to prevent aggression, the Labour Party is profoundly pacific. It regards all war as an evil, and can admit the use of armed force only if a greater evil is to be avoided. There has, however, been a tendency in the past, among some Socialists, to consider that there was something wrong in even attempting to understand the problems of defence. I have even been rebuked for making suggestions which were intended to make the defence services more efficient. My correspondent seemed to have a muddled idea that an inefficient army was somehow less wicked than an efficient one. It is, I believe, essential that Labour men and women should understand what modern war means, and should make up their minds as to what their attitude is to be on problems of defence.

Armaments are an expression of policy. What armed forces it is necessary to have are determined by the policy which is pursued by the Government both at home and abroad. Where a Government rests upon the consent of the governed, it will require only a small force as the ultimate sanction for its authority in a country where resort to violence is very exceptional. Where, however, there is a dictatorship, it is necessary for the Government to have always ready sufficient forces to prevent its being overthrown by violence, for in authoritarian States the only method of change is forcible revolution. In this country law and order are preserved by an unarmed police force, and, although there are in reserve the armed forces of the Crown, their use has been for many years extremely rare. It is, however, no use blinking the fact that in the last resort a Government must be prepared to defend its authority if challenged by force. A Labour Government, if faced with an attempt to seize power by violence, would be bound to use all the forces at its command to protect democracy. It is, therefore, obliged to see that the armed forces upon which in the last resort its power depends are loyal, efficient, and adequate. The fact that the Government, as the constitutional Government of the country, will have the support not only of its own actual supporters, but of all law-abiding citizens against any attempt to seize power by force, does not relieve it of the duty of seeing that the armed forces are sufficient, but only affects the amount which it is necessary to maintain. Great Britain is also a member of a Commonwealth of Nations and part of a great Empire. It has been for years the main repository of armed force for the preservation of internal order throughout this Empire which comprises peoples in every stage of civilisation. The amount of force required for imperial police work depends, again, on the extent to which the Government in every part of the Empire rests on the consent of the governed. It also depends on the law-abidingness of the populations in various parts of the Empire. Where there are people living under protection of British power who are liable to be attacked by uncivilised peoples only restrained by their knowledge of the existence of that power, it is impossible, without grave breach of faith, suddenly to withdraw that protection. The defence problem of Great Britain, from the point of view of internal security alone, involves the maintenance of armed forces.

The Labour Party policy in regard to colonies, mandated territories, and protectorates, which I have dealt with elsewhere, and the gradual extension of self-government to all, will tend to reduce the amount of armed force which must be retained as a central reserve for emergencies. The amount of armaments for internal, as for external, use depends on policy.

The defence of Great Britain, the British Commonwealth, and the British Empire against external attack is a duty of Government, whatever may be its political complexion. How this is to be secured depends primarily on policy. If an imperialist policy is pursued whereby Great Britain claims to retain for its own use and for the use of the Dominions, excluding all the rest of the world, one quarter of the surface of the earth, enormous forces will be required. The pursuit of such a policy is, in my view, purely anarchic. The Labour Party rejects altogether the conception of empire whereby the world is parcelled out between Great Powers with their territories and spheres of influence sharply defined. It stands for a world commonwealth, and for the enjoyment by all of the resources of the world.

I do not believe that British possessions all over the world can be defended by national armaments. Britain has never fought a great war single-handed. The policy of isolation is hopeless from the point of view of defence. The Labour Party also rejects a policy of alliances and the balance of power. It stands firm for collective security through the League of Nations.

An attempt is often made to draw a distinction between national defence and collective security. There are those who suggest that a Government must provide for the defence of its own territories, and then, as a kind of extra precaution, enter into an agreement for collective security. This is, I believe, a complete fallacy. I do not believe that it is possible for this country to provide for its defence in isolation. The only possible security is through the renunciation of aggression and the close binding together of a number of States in an agreement for mutual assistance which will give an absolute assurance that aid will be forthcoming. Given a sufficient strength within this league of collective security aggression will not take place. But it is obviously a condition of the effectiveness of such a method that all cases of aggression against any member State will be considered as aggression against all.

There seems, also, in the minds of many people an idea that the safety of Great Britain can be assured through collective agreement, but that the British Empire must be left to be defended by the arms of Britain alone. I do not think this is practical. An attack on any part of the British Empire or the Commonwealth must necessarily involve Great Britain. It can only be undertaken by a major Power or Powers. The attack cannot be isolated. It follows, therefore, that in any scheme of collective security the British Empire must come in as a unit. The Dominions have, of course, the right to decide their own course of action, but if they do not come into such a League, and seek to contract out of its obligations, they will be at the same time lessening their own protection. The mutual assistance which membership of the British Commonwealth of nations affords is enlarged by co-operation in the wider unity of the League.

It is for this reason that I believe that an effective agreement for collective security must be inclusive, so as to provide for the defence of all its members against all aggression. The policy of the Labour Party of extending the principle of the mandate to all colonial possessions will naturally place them under the protection of the League. I have stated that the forces of a league of collective security must be adequate to prevent aggressive action. The amount required is naturally determined by the strength of the potential aggressors. Great Britain will naturally have to provide her share of the forces necessary to repel aggression.

The Labour Party has always recognised this.

It has never, as opponents suggest, sought a cheap security at the expense of others. As a matter of fact, the proposals for the level of British armaments by Conservative or " National " Governments have always been put forward on the ground that they were necessary for the defence of this country, without any reference to the existence of other forces which would, under the League system, be available to assist against aggression. The truth is, that up to the present the British Government has never attempted to make collective security a reality, and their technical advisers have continued to think in terms of national defence in isolation.

The amount of the forces necessary in a system of collective security is not to be arrived at by adding together a number of separate navies, armies, and air forces and presenting the total in comparison with the forces at the disposal of a potential aggressor. Without a consideration of geographical disposition, and of the factor of time in mobilisation, such a comparison is illusory. Without strategic co-ordination an apparently stronger force may actually be inferior to a smaller one which enjoys unity of command. The weakness of the League hitherto has been that there has been no real consideration of the organisation of force as a sanction against aggression. The League has consisted of a number of States pursuing national aims and commanding purely national forces. If a real system of collective security is to be built up, there will be required a far greater subordination of individual units to the whole. It is a realisation of the weakness of a number of national forces as a guarantee of peace that has led the Labour Party to support the policy of an international air police force. Whether one is looking to an ultimate all-embracing co-operative commonwealth or is considering only the immediate problem of making the League strong enough to prevent aggression, it is, I believe, vital that there should be unified direction of the forces of the League. The present weakness of the democratic States in face of Fascist aggression is not due to their actual inferiority in strength. On the contrary even to-day they are actually stronger, and they are immeasurably better off in war potential—that is, in resources of personnel and material. The non-Fascist States command a very great proportion of all the supplies of materials used in war. The World War showed the immense importance of the economic factor which did in fact decide the issue. It is only disunity that makes the peaceful States appear weak. I have stated above my belief that a Socialist Government in this country could rebuild the League and make it an instrument for world peace and world prosperity. It could also make it strong enough to resist all aggression and thus establish conditions in which a new world order could be founded. A Labour Government coming into power will have to deal with the state of affairs which it finds existing. Its armament policy will depend on its foreign policy. The greater the success of the former the more rapid will be the progress towards world disarmament.

In the meantime it is necessary to consider what general principles should be applied to the organisation of the defence forces of this country. Two things must be considered: first, how most efficiently and economically to provide such forces as are required; and, second, how to secure that the armed forces of the Crown are kept in the closest touch with the nation. In this country ever since the time of the Commonwealth there has been great care taken that there should not be any possibility of action against the people by the armed forces. The Army Annual Act is a reminder of the suspicion which this country has always had of standing armies as potential enemies to liberty. As a matter of fact, with the single exception of the Curragh incident, there has been no occasion on which the armed forces have endeavoured to pursue a policy adverse to the Government of the day. There is no reason to believe that there is any likelihood of the armed forces of the Crown acting in any other way when Labour is in power, but that is no reason why every effort should not be taken to see that the armed forces are so organised as not to form a potential danger to democracy.

ORGANISATION OF DEFENCE

The organisation of the defence forces is the result of the geography and history of this country. Its island position has led the predominant consideration to be the maintenance of the command of the sea, and therefore the primacy of the Navy over the Army. Historical events have led to the subordination of the military to the civil element.

To both factors is due the fact that the armed forces of the Crown have, except very occasionally, been raised on a voluntary basis. The country has depended for its defence on a professional Navy, Army, and, latterly, Air Force, with unpaid voluntary formations as a second line. The armed forces have been to some extent kept in the background. The nation has not been militarised. On the other hand, the forces have never been democratised, the officers having always preponderatingly been drawn from the wealthier classes. Except for the World War the contests in which Great Britain has been involved have been fought mainly by professionals. The nation has not been mobilised for war. In the World War for the first time the whole force of the nation was mobilised, and it was then realised that in any major contest the whole nation is involved, and that success in war depends not only on the armed forces but on the economic organisation behind them.

Professional soldiers and sailors are for the most part conservative in their mental habits, relying on old traditions and resentful of innovations. This is especially so in time of peace, when the higher command is staffed with old men whose ideas have been formed on past experience. To this conservatism is added the professional interests of those whose prospects will be affected by change. A good instance of this is afforded by what happened at the end of the World War. Every effort was made to get back to the pre-war position. Each service endeavoured to establish its own autonomy and followed its own strategic policies. The advent of air power had, however, altered the whole problem of defence. Britain was now in an extremely vulnerable position and liable to an attack that might mean disaster at a few hours notice. The whole basis of pre-war defence strategy had changed, but there has been no sign that this was recognised in the provision made for defence. The speeches of Service Ministers supporting their estimates might have been written in the days of two-dimensional warfare. The Navy continues to be regarded as the first line of defence and to get the lion's share of money. The three Services are independent, and despite a certain amount of eyewash there has been no real strategical co-ordination. At the Disarmament Conference the experts from the Services looked after their Service interests. When rearmament was embarked upon, increases were largely quantitative rather than qualitative. The plan seemed to consist of making additions to an existing structure which was the result of demobilisation at the end of the World War rather than anything planned to meet new conditions.

The first thing a Labour Government would have to do would be to break down the exclusiveness of the three Services and create a real Ministry of Defence and a defence staff trained to think in terms of three elements. It would have to consider the amount of armaments and their distribution as a whole considered in relation to the problem of defence. This amount would necessarily be affected by the policy pursued in foreign affairs. But defence is not just a matter of the provision of a certain amount of fighting men and warlike material. The vital thing is the maintenance of civilian as well as military morale, for the conditions of modern warfare are such as to expose the civilian population to the danger of attack. Defence also demands the mobilisation of the economic resources of the whole country.

It follows, therefore, that the supreme authority for defence must be civilian, and that the professional fighters must understand the problems which have to be faced by the civil Government.

The organisation of a country for defence involves the planning of its resources.

In the necessities of modern warfare there is at once a great danger and a great opportunity. There is a danger lest under the excuse of organising the nation for defence and security liberty may be destroyed and the Corporate State introduced. The greater the danger, the greater the opportunity of persuading people to accept all kinds of restrictions. On the other hand, the plain needs of the situation require the introduction of orderly planning in the place of chaotic competition. This, in effect, means the adoption of a great deal of collectivism and the firm supersession of vested interests. It is precisely here that Capitalist Governments break down, because they depend on private interests which put profits before anything else and look upon the nation's necessity as their opportunity. There is, therefore, great danger in planning by a Capitalist Government. It will inevitably mean the suppression of the rights of the individual as a citizen and as a worker in industry. It will be dominated by private interests, especially by those mainly responsible for munitions production. Discipline will be imposed from above. In the name of liberty and democracy, freedom will be suppressed.

A Labour Government, on the contrary, will take over the private manufacture of arms and munitions, and its basis of organisation will be the discipline which is imposed willingly by the people themselves in a matter in which they have a common concern, knowing that they are not to be exploited on behalf of the interests of a section. The planning which a Labour Government will put into effect will not be something imposed on the people solely in order to attain an efficient war machine, but will be aimed at securing the highest standard of life possible for all, but incidentally such planning will make the nation far more able to stand up to the conditions of war if war should come. The first condition necessary for a nation is that its citizens should be fit. The British Capitalist Government has not even had the intelligence to realise that sweated conditions mean a C3 nation. The next essential condition is that there should be a high civilian morale. This cannot be obtained unless the State is based on social justice. The utilisation of the resources of the nation cannot be secured while vested interests are allowed to have precedence of the national need. The location of industry from the strategic as well as from the social and economic point of view involves definite planning. The vital service of transportation must be co-ordinated under public control. The organisation of food production and the control of imports and exports were shown to be necessary during the World War.

NATIONALISATION OF ARMAMENT MANUFACTURE

The nationalisation of the armaments industry is one of the most important points in Labour's programme. There are many people outside the ranks of Labour who are convinced that the scandal of profit-making in armaments should cease. They have an instinctive revulsion against the conception of private individuals benefiting financially from the sale of weapons of war. During recent years, too, the methods of some firms in securing orders have been exposed with devastating effect. It has been found that sales have been effected in foreign countries by bribery of important personages, and that war scares have been deliberately started in order to create a demand for armaments. I have not space here to go fully into the case against the private armaments firms, but I think there is no doubt but what it has in large measure been proven. If, indeed, only a fraction of the accusations are substantiated there is an urgent case upon moral grounds for the removal of armament manufacture from the arena of private profit.

There are many people who will agree with me thus far, but will argue that they do not believe that the State can be trusted to manufacture armaments efficiently, and that it is worth while to suffer a twinge of conscience every now and then in order to ensure that we get all the armaments that we need. This argument cannot bear examination, however, in the light of the experience of the last war. Time and again the private arms firms were unable to fulfil their contracts. Even when they did fulfil them it was at a price out of all reason. In brief, when it came to the crucial point, and the country put the claims of the armament manufacturers to the test, it was found that they were incapable of the rapid and efficient expansion in war-time, which is said to be one of their most useful characteristics, as opposed to Government munition factories. It was found, too, that they were ready, in many cases, to take full advantage of the nation's sudden need for arms, by charging exorbitant prices, which were only brought down after a stringent Government enquiry had been instituted.

Yet another argument that is adduced against the nationalisation of the armaments industry is that it is exceedingly difficult to say what exactly constitutes " armament." In these days, so the argument runs, almost everything, including food and clothing, to say nothing of iron and steel, can be considered as part of the nation's equipment in time of war, and are therefore in a sense "armaments." While there may be a superficial appearance of truth in this argument, I would answer, in the first place, that the French Government have recently taken over a large number of firms engaged in the manufacture of armaments. They have, it seems, interpreted the word "armaments" as meaning only those articles whose use is exclusively for war purposes. They have, indeed, been so strict in their interpretation that they have in some cases taken over a single section of a factory, and left the rest in private hands. In spite of this, however, the French Government is now the owner on behalf of the people of a large number of armament factories, including the well-known firm of Schneider Creusot.

This particular argument does not, however, carry very great weight with me. As a Socialist I consider that nationalisation should extend far beyond the limits of armament firms, and it would not worry me at all if a few firms not strictly to be classed as armament makers were taken over in the process. The main thing is to see that the stain of profit-making in human lives should be removed once and for all from our country.

DEMOCRATISATION

In the organisation of the fighting Services themselves, there are two prime necessities: the application of common sense, and democratisation. In all the mass of waste which occurred during the last war two examples stand out: first, the waste of human life through the refusal to apply common sense when common sense was in conflict with preconceived ideas; and, second, the waste of the brain-power of the nation by restricting staff appointments to the regular officer and thus failing to use the first-class ability which was available. Few people would deny that brains were to a large extent suspect in the pre-war Army. Orthodoxy was the rule. The problems which have to be met by the higher command in the future require a very wide outlook. It is not enough to understand purely military or naval problems. War now involves every activity of a nation, and the wider the contact between officers and people engaged in other fields the better. What is required especially is that there should be wide opportunity for discussion and the consideration of the constantly changing problems of defence. It is noticeable that to-day officers who show power of original thought seldom last long in the Services.

The restriction of the officer cadre to the limits of one social class narrows the field of selection, and has obvious political dangers—as indicated above. It also makes the gulf between officers and men very wide. This is not to suggest that there is not good feeling between officers and men, but that there is a wide gulf of class distinction and way of living which makes a bar to promotion from the ranks. Intelligent officers realise that the conditions of war have changed. The old conception of masses of ignorant men led by officers of a superior class is out of date. The fighting man to-day is called upon to act as an individual. He is tending to become a highly skilled technician in charge of complicated machinery. There is no room for the stupid man in modern war. To alter the basis of an officer cadre is not easy, and must necessarily take time if the machine is to function during the change, but the democratisation of the fighting Services must be taken in hand by a Labour Government. They will, I believe, find a surprising amount of support for it among the officers of the Services.

A beginning should be made by insisting that all officers should be drawn from the ranks, and that all entrance to the Services should be through the ranks. Colleges such as Woolwich, Sandhurst, Cranwell, and Dartford should be filled by likely young men from the ranks, selected for their qualities, and not for their class connections. The training should be definitely on university lines. The conditions of officers and men should be brought nearer together. The caste barrier should be broken down and there should be comradeship off parade. The mess and the ward-room should no longer be annexes to the country house. The man who enters the Service should be able to live on his pay and look forward to employment on reverting to civil life, and to an adequate pension on retirement. Probably there would have to be a certain amount of retirement of older officers who could not accommodate themselves to the new conditions, and a promotion of the younger officers with more active minds. This in itself would be a great advantage to the Services, for the higher positions tend to-day to be staffed by men whose minds are out of date. Given good conditions, I believe that there need be no great disturbance, and that there would be no question of disloyalty on account of the political complexion of the Government. There should, on the other hand, be no attempt to influence the Services to take a particular political view. Nothing is worse than the political general or admiral. It is a major indictment against the Conservative Party that they allowed themselves to tamper with the loyalty of the Army at the time of the Home Rule controversy. The fighting Services should contain men of all political views, entitled to hold them as citizens, but, like the civil service, there should be no question of party affiliations conflicting with loyal service to whatever Government is in power.

The armed forces of the Crown should be in their opinions as nearly akin as possible to the civilian population. Their members should not be a body segregated from the rest of the population.

On the contrary, the closest contact should be maintained.

It is one of the natural incidents of a Capitalist Government that public advantage often means unmerited hardship on individuals. A Labour Government pursuing a successful foreign policy of peace will find itself sooner or later in a position to reduce its armed forces. There should be no question of making the personnel of the Services suffer by wholesale dismissals without provision being made for the livelihood of those affected. Here again the problem of dealing with the personnel rendered redundant by disarmament can only be dealt with effectively by a Government which is pursuing the Socialist policy of utilising the resources of the country for the good of all.

A Labour Government, in organising the defence forces of the country, will, as I have stated, be doing so definitely on the basis of providing the forces necessary for the preservation of peace through the League of Nations. It will not therefore be engaged in organising national defence forces, but international. It will be working for the abolition of national forces and for their replacement by an international police force.

INTERNATIONAL POLICE

I hold that a Labour Government must immediately take the initiative in the League for the formation of an international police force. As long as the force behind the League consists of a number of separate national armies, navies, and air forces, there will be influences which are really adverse to peace. Those in command of national forces must inevitably think and plan to a large extent in terms of national defence. They must create and maintain a national morale. A Labour Government must endeavour to build up a super-loyalty to peace and to create a force which is international in outlook. I have not space here to develop the arguments for an international air force, or to sketch, even in outline, how it should be composed. Much work has already been done on working out the plans for such a development. I can only say that I do not believe that the scheme of an international air force is chimerical. I think that it is supremely practical. I myself believe that even a start among a limited number of nations in this direction would be an immense advance. With it necessarily goes the internationalisation of civil aviation. I believe that the formation of a real international aviation service might be a most powerful factor in creating international sentiment, provided that it was done under Socialist influences. If the most powerful offensive weapons in the world were manned by men drawn from many nations who would in their service create an *esprit de corps* based on common service in the interests of humanity, and if the great services of international transport also passed out of national control, a real constructive step towards world peace would have been taken. Not only would the world be acquiring a great common service, but it would be creating a cadre of men with a loyalty towards humanity, transcending the narrower loyalty of nationalism.

In the meantime, the Labour Party has to face the actual conditions of to-day when in Opposition. There is some misunderstanding as to the Party's attitude. The Labour Party is opposed to the policy of the National Government in seeking security by piling up huge competitive armaments. It can only tolerate armaments as a necessary support for a policy of collective security. It is fully alive to the dangers which exist in Europe to-day owing to the aggressive policy of the Fascist Powers, but it has no confidence in the will of a Capitalist Government to oppose them. There is every indication that the policy pursued is an attempt to play the old game of alliances based on the maintenance of the balance of power. To say that what the Government is doing is necessary for the defence of the country is to beg the whole question. I do not believe that the entry into a competition in arms will give security. On the contrary, I think that it is leading straight to the disaster of another world war.

The Labour Party, therefore, has steadily opposed the rearmament policy of the Government, not on the ground that the level of armaments of two years ago is adequate, or even that the present scale is not excessive, but because it is impossible to tell what the scale of armaments should be in the absence of any sound foreign policy. To make the scale dependent upon what other Powers are doing is to engage in a mere armaments race.

Opposition to an armaments programme does not, however, involve the denial of any armaments whatever, any more than an objection to the policy of the Home Office involves the abolition of the police force. A Government which is supported by a majority of the electors is entitled to carry out its policy. An Opposition will do all it can to convince the electors that this policy is wrong. Beyond this we enter into the sphere of revolutionary action. I have stated above the conditions in which I think that unconstitutional action is justified. The occasion may arise when it is right and necessary for even a minority to resist by every means in its power the policy pursued by the majority, but an insistence that because a minority believes a policy to be wrong it should therefore obstruct its implementation is undemocratic and leads to the conditions of the Corporate State.

The Labour Party will continue to oppose the Government's arms policy because it believes it to be wrong and dangerous. It will oppose every attempt to destroy democracy and liberty under the pretence of safeguarding the country. It will make it unmistakably plain to the Government that the national unity essential to success in war will not be forthcoming while the Government pursues a policy of alliance and the balance of power.

CHAPTER XI

PROSPECT

I HAVE NOW LOOKED at the Labour Party in retrospect. I have given some account of its origins and of the forces which gave birth to it. I have described its organisation, discussed some of its internal difficulties, indicated its principles and ultimate aims, and dealt in some detail with its immediate policy in home and foreign affairs. What of the future? It is difficult to look far ahead, and very dangerous to prophesy. We are living in a world of rapid change. Immense forces for good and evil have been released. There is a new generation about to take its full part in shaping the future, which has been subjected to influences very different from those experienced by the men and women of my own generation. It may well be that my anticipations fail to take into consideration the effect of the changes of social habit which I see proceeding, and that I give too much weight to past precedents. Yet it is necessary to try to make some kind of forecast, if only for the next few years. In my view the future of civilisation hangs in the balance, and the people of this country have it in their power to play a decisive part.

I do not believe that the only choice before us is the acceptance of Fascism or Communism. I do not think that Britain must follow the Moscow or the Berlin road. Those two roads have certain features in common. They are straight, narrow, and artificial. They drive through the landscape of humanity with little apparent reference to its contours or to the graces of the countryside which have been derived from the past. Those who journey along them attain a very high rate of speed, and they scorn old-fashioned meandering paths. There are many casualties on that account. A high rate of speed may give great pleasure to those who control the machines, but it may mean a vast amount of discomfort to the driven. The real question is, to what place will those who complete the journey arrive?—if, indeed, they do arrive, for there is a great possibility of a terrible catastrophe on the way. One may ask, too, in what kind of condition will those who journey be like when the road has been traversed? One can give no certain answer to these questions, whether one considers the travellers on the Moscow or on the Berlin highways.

I have already set out my objections to the Totalitarian State, whether formed on the Fascist or Communist model, and I will not repeat them here. I do not think that it is desirable as an ideal or necessary as a stage in human development. In my view the Totalitarian State is not an advance in civilisation but a retrogression. It has been adopted by peoples who are politically and socially immature. They have not grasped the fact that the essential condition for an advanced civilisation is tolerance, and that a society in which men and women of differing views on many subjects can live together in peace and harmony is a higher type than one in which all must conform to a single pattern. The achievement of the Totalitarian State involves the use of force, and its continuance requires the use of the same methods. The one thing indispensable is an all-pervading police service. While this continues there is no freedom, and until it is abolished the experiment in Russia will not attract the majority of the British people.

It is, in my view, the strength, not the weakness, of Britain which allows of wide tolerance and freedom, permitting people to disagree on matters of vital importance and yet to continue to live together in friendly intercourse. To exchange this for a society in which everything is subordinated to a ruthless class warfare would be a retrograde step. Avoiding both Fascism and Communism, this country, I believe, can afford to the world an example of how society can adapt itself to new conditions and base itself on new principles without breach of continuity and without violence and intolerance. We have in the past to a great extent avoided the civil wars which have done such a vast amount of harm in other countries. It is, I think, a false reading of history to think that what has happened elsewhere must necessarily happen in this country. It has not been so in the past. It was, I think, characteristic of Britain that, on the only occasion on which there arose a military dictatorship, the dictator was a man who strove continually for tolerance and sought unceasingly to rid himself of the burden of absolute power and to return to the ways of constitutionalism. Cromwell was as English as Mussolini is Italian.

I think that nations tend to follow very closely their national traditions. Italy has frequently been the arena for faction fights and proscriptions. The Fascist methods are nothing new to the descendants of the Guelfs and Ghibellines. Military despotism has been a feature of German history. It is still a question whether or not Russia will return to the autocracy which she has so long endured. It is my faith that Britain will be true to her traditions, and that, despite the profound differences that separate the supporters of Socialism and Capitalism, the changes which are necessary will be brought about without bloodshed and violence. It is the genius of the British people to modify and adapt old institutions to new purposes. I think that the same process which has been followed in the past will be employed in the future for changing the social and economic structure of this country.

I believe that the Labour Party is the instrument whereby this change will be effected. Typically British, the Labour Party has shown its power of adaption to new conditions and new purposes. At its inception it was a party representing almost entirely organised Labour. Its programme was sectional, not national. It has since then developed into a national party, open to all, and has a policy which embraces every phase of national life. In its earlier days it would have been a fair criticism to have said that it could not aspire to power because its appeal was too narrow. It is not true to-day. Increasingly it draws its strength from men and women of all classes of society. Its achievement of power does not depend on an alteration in the quality of its adherents, but in their quantity. It has to convert to its faith many millions of workers who still cling to Capitalism. It has to persuade many members of the classes which depend in the main on their own work for their livelihood that true community of interest is based on fellowship in service, not on participation in profits.

There is, I believe, an ever-growing number of people who, although comparatively well-to-do, are yet profoundly dissatisfied with the Capitalist system. There are technicians and business managers who find that their efforts lead only to frustration. When they invent new machinery or introduce improvements into production, they more often than not find that as a result of their labours a number of workers have been thrown out of their jobs, while not infrequently the increased production which they have effected cannot be absorbed because of the maldistribution of purchasing power.

There is also a realisation that in modern large-scale industry there is but little chance of a man becoming his own master. He is apt to be only a servant of a company. He realises that he might as well serve the community instead of a certain number of profit-takers. The uncertainty of private enterprise which was so manifest during the great depression has made more attractive the prospects of serving the State or the municipality. But I think that a more powerful motive which is bringing into the ranks of labour so many individuals from the better-off classes is a realisation of the immoral and unjust basis of Capitalism. The social conscience speaks loudly to-day. Where formerly it impelled people of goodwill to give to charity, it now leads them to examine into the system which produces injustice. Where formerly they were content to deal with results, they now seek to remove causes.

The fact is that the ranks of the supporters of

the Capitalist system are constantly being thinned by the desertion of those who have lost faith in it. Many of these find their way into the ranks of Labour. There is, however, a great body of citizens who, while unable to give their former support to Capitalism, still fear to accept Socialism and all its implications. I believe that they will come to realise that there is no alternative. At present they hesitate partly through prejudice and partly through misunderstanding.

It is the task of the Labour Party to win over to its side all these elements which are still uncertain of their position. To do this involves a receptivity on the part of the Labour Party itself. It does not in my view involve watering down Labour's Socialist creed in order to attract new adherents who cannot accept the full Socialist faith. On the contrary I believe that it is only a clear and bold policy that will attract their support. It is not the preaching of a feeble kind of Liberalism that is required, but a frank statement of the full Socialist faith in terms which will be understood.

I do not believe that there is need for a great change in the constitution of the Labour Party. Its basis in organised Labour must remain. The complaint that the Labour Party is bossed by a few Trade Union officials is untrue. The constitution of the Party is democratic. Individual membership is open to all. I anticipate that in the course of the next few years there will be a rapid increase of individual membership which will give the local Labour Parties an even greater influence than that which they now possess. I hope that the Party will continue to be a party of the rank and file, and that those who enter its ranks will accept the conditions and discipline of democracy. There is not, and should not be, a royal road to influence in the Labour movement.

The Labour Party is what its members make it.

The future of the Labour Party depends on two things—its success in winning power in this country, and the way in which it uses that power when it has been obtained.

I am convinced that the achievement of power in the near future is possible if every member of the Party will do his share in making converts. The country is ready for a great step forward. There is not to-day, as there was when I first entered the movement, a widespread and active opposition to the practical proposals which Socialists put forward. The majority of the people have become accustomed to a large measure of State direction. They have seen the principle of public ownership and management applied to great undertakings such as the British Broadcasting Corporation, the London Passenger Transport Board, and the Post Office. The word "Socialistic" has lost much of its terror. Where the Socialist creed is expounded simply and clearly it gains adherents in all classes. This, however, is not to say that there is not much spade work still to be done. The obstacles to success are formidable.

In considering the future it is well to realise the strength of the forces opposed to the Labour Party. The most powerful of these is, as it always has been, the lack of imagination of the majority of people. This is not realised by those who have seen the light. They appreciate so clearly the developments which are going on in the world. They trace results to the underlying causes. They know that in Socialism they have the key which will unlock the treasure house of a better world, and do not realise the inability of so many people to look beyond the narrow bounds of their everyday experience. There is a vast number of people to whom all existence is a series of facts. They never attempt to relate these facts to any consistent theory. Much earnest propaganda is wasted through failure to appreciate the psychology of the average elector.

In modern business the most highly developed art is that of the salesman. It matters not whether it is a patent medicine, a motor-car, a policy of insurance, or a newspaper, those who are interested in their sales have to make a careful study of the right method of approach. In the world of to-day the citizen is subjected from morning to night to a heavy barrage of propaganda which is directed to his eyes and his ears. In one way or another all this propaganda has its effect on the minds of men and women. The wireless, the cinema, and the newspaper above all, are instruments of great potency. They take the place of the old-fashioned agencies of the book, the sermon, and the speech. They mould the minds of the rising generation. These instruments are to a very great extent either consciously or unconsciously on the side of those who support the present order of society. They build up an atmosphere which it is very difficult for the Socialist to penetrate. Anyone who has been brought up in a conventional home will know the difficult adjustment necessary for the member of the family who chooses another path. He has to effect a revolution in all his conceptions. He has to part with the class prejudices which he has taken in as naturally as the air he breathes. This atmosphere is the first line of defence of the Capitalist system against its assailants. But it is reinforced when there is a General Election by the skilful use of every kind of instrument of propaganda which can be brought into play. It is here that the command of large sums of money and of skilled technicians in the art of publicity count heavily. A great deal of the art of salesmanship lies in constant repetition. A half-truth or a downright lie can be repeated in hundreds of periodicals and can be presented under many attractive guises, so that only those who really think seriously on political matters are armed against its attack.

Another strong force which is utilised against Labour is fear. To a greater or less extent at every General Election an appeal has been made to the fears of the ordinary man. Sometimes they are scared by the spectacle of the " horror of Communism in Russia." On another occasion they are told to tremble for the safety of their savings. The dangers which may come from an outbreak of war will be used with complete unscrupulousness to persuade the electors to vote for " safety first." Where these specific terrors are not adduced, there is still the general appeal to timidity. The elector will be persuaded that old ways are safer, that it is dangerous to make new experiments. This makes an extremely effective appeal to people who live in a country where there has been for years a developed civilisation. In a highly industrialised Capitalist country where there are big concentrations of capital and large-scale undertakings, and where security of economic position opens the door to modest comfort, the tendency to seek for a safe job is far greater than in low-standard countries, or in those where the pioneer spirit is still active. It is no good telling a man with a suburban villa on the hire-purchase system and a routine job of £3 10s. a week that he has nothing to lose but his chains. It may be that he has chains, but he hugs them.

Finally one must face the all-important fact that there is a very long road to be travelled before this country can be cleansed from the snobbery and mean ideals which are still widely accepted. In Britain there is the strongest Capitalist class in the world, and on the whole it is also the cleverest. It is unlikely to adopt the crude and brutal methods which have been used in other countries. It is generally too clever to show its hand very obviously or to outrage human feeling. It uses the language of reform and peace and democracy, and gains its ends, not by playing upon the worst human instincts, but by persuading the ordinary decent person that it is going to realise all his highest ideals by other ways than those of the reformers and Socialists.

While it is right to face up to the forces that make against the success of the Labour Party, it is not necessary to exaggerate them or to minimise the influences which make for that success. I believe that it is impossible to contend against the tendencies which are making more necessary every day a planned society, and which render it out of the question to continue a class society based on gross inequalities of wealth. Capitalism is manifestly failing. A temporary recovery from depression gives it a short new lease of life, but the next depression is deeper than its predecessor. The increasingly high standards of education of the workers are making the task of the Socialist easier. Developments of mass production are tending to break down barriers of social habit which used to be the strongest supports to class distinctions. The confidence which used to belong to the supporters of the existing order is being steadily sapped. But the future of the Labour Party depends, first and foremost, on the idealism, the devotion, and the intelligence of the rank and file of its adherents. The existence in this country of thousands of men and women who give freely of their time and labour for the cause in which they believe is the thing which has enabled the workers, despite all the advantages of money, education, economic power, and social privilege which belong to their opponents, to create a political party able to contend for power. It is this army of active Socialists which will in due time achieve power and create the Britain which they desire. The deciding factor, to my mind, will not be leadership or the exact theories which are held to be orthodox Socialism. It will not be the brilliance of particular individuals. The thing which will secure the triumph of Labour will be the demonstration by Socialists in their lives that they have a high ideal and live up to it. People are converted more by what they see Socialists are than by what they hear them say. Here is the responsibility which lies upon everyone in the movement.

The daily actions of professing Socialists are either helping or hindering the achievement which all desire.

The thing which does more harm than anything else is the lack of unity among Socialists and the bitterness which is imported into these dissensions. I am no enemy of plain speaking, and I think that it is stupid and dishonest to try to make a superficial unity where there is really profound difference of aim and method, but unnecessary suspicions and personal attacks play into the hands of our enemies.

There remains to be considered the way in which the Labour Party uses power when it has received a mandate from the electors. I am convinced that whenever this mandate has been given, the Labour programme must be carried out with the utmost vigour and resolution. To delay dealing with essentials would be fatal. To show irresolution or cowardice would be to invite defeat. A Labour Government should make it quite plain that it will suffer nothing to hinder it in carrying out the popular will. In all great enterprises it is the first steps that are difficult, and it is the way in which these are taken that makes the difference between success or failure. A Labour Government, not in a spirit of malice or revenge, but with the greatest regard for justice to all, must resolutely set about its task of rebuilding the life of this country on the principles of liberty, equality, and social justice, and of joining with other nations to create a world Commonwealth.

THE END